Michael Glover

111 Places
in Sheffield
That You
Shouldn't Miss

Photographs by Richard Anderson

T0343656

emons:

In memory of Stanley Cook,
poet of Sheffield and my teacher at
Firth Park Grammar School

For John Birtwhistle, Mireille Berthoud and Norman West,
without whose unstinting generosity and kindness this book
would never have been written.

© Emons Verlag GmbH
All rights reserved
© All photographs Richard Anderson, except:
Portrait Bust of John Ruskin, Joseph Edgar Boehm (1834–1890),
plaster cast, 1879, courtesy Collection of the Guild of St George,
Museums Sheffield; Buffalo Bull programme image courtesy National
Fairground Archive, University of Sheffield; *Sheffield Year Knife*
courtesy Ken Hawley Collection Trust, Sheffield; portrait of Patrick Moore
courtesy Rocket; *Heppo Scissorhands* (at Ernest Wright and Sons)
© Jason Heponstall; *River Don Engine* and *The Sheffield Simplex*
courtesy Sheffield Industrial Museums Trust; *The Buffer Girls* (1919)
by Sir William Rothenstein, courtesy Museums Sheffield; Edward Carpenter's
sandals courtesy Sheffield City Archives: Carpenter/W/1; thanks to St Marie's
Cathedral for permission to photograph; George Fullard's *Walking Man*
and Fullard sculptures in Upper Chapel Forecourt, courtesy Museums
Sheffield and reproduced with permission from the George Fullard Estate;
The Cutting Edge Sculpture courtesy Sheffield City Council
© Cover motif: private
Edited by Alison Lester
Design: Eva Kraskes, based on a design
by Lübbeke | Naumann | Thoben
Maps: altancicek.design, www.altancicek.de
Printing and binding: Grafisches Centrum Cuno, Calbe
Printed in Germany 2024
ISBN 978-3-7408-2348-1
Revised fifth edition, June 2024

Guidebooks for Locals & Experienced Travelers
Join us in uncovering new places around the world at:
www.111places.com

Foreword

Welcome to Sheffield, the under-sung city once described by George Orwell as the ugliest town in the world. He had spent just three days here. The truth is quite otherwise. Sheffield is a place of unanticipated delights which have as much to do with the rural as the urban – a significant proportion of greater Sheffield is contained within some of the most dramatic countryside in England, and the drama of its landscape is one of Sheffield's glories.

This is also a restive place, independent of spirit, cussed in character, a place which has always had singular opinions. Where does it come from, this bullish spiritedness? Associated since the 12th century with metalworking and the cutlery trade (the poet Geoffrey Chaucer refers to a Sheffield knife in *The Reeve's Tale*), by the middle of the 19th century the city's name had become synonymous with the mass-production of steel. Perhaps it was those cutlers who gave Sheffield its very special character. Often working alone or in small groups, opinionated, highly skilled, literate, these 'little mesters' contributed to the fact that Sheffield had such Jacobin leanings – it was a great supporter of the French Revolution. In fact, Sheffield was a very radical place for much of its history, often at loggerheads with masters of church and state. And yet until 1832 it had no parliamentary representatives whatsoever, and it did not become a city until 1897.

Mass employment in the steel industry ended in the 1980s, thanks to the machinations of the Thatcher government. The coal industry died too. And yet Sheffield thrives again – as a place of varied and innovative creation. The world's finest surgical instruments are made here. The Gripple, an ingenious wire-joiner, is a Sheffield invention. Sheffield also is one of the beer capitals of the world, and its music-making will beckon you onto the dance floor.

111 Places

1 Abbeydale Industrial Hamlet

Small-scale industry from muscle and sweat

This entire industrial hamlet of grimy, sturdily brick-built, modest-looking two-storey cottages and workshops dating from the 18th and 19th centuries, loosely arranged around a straggly open courtyard, with a five-acre mill dam at its back to power four great water-wheels, is a wonderfully intact survival of Sheffield's heritage as a place of the making of hand-forged scythes and edge tools with the aid of fire and water and brute muscle. The entire place is self-sufficient: a scythe or a grass hook could be made here from first to last. Everything is of a piece. It looks as if the workers walked away one day, quite casually, leaving everything as it once was. In fact, it was last a working hamlet in the 1930s.

Stare at the boots in the grate of an 18th-century worker's cottage. There's a warming pan on the bed and a pot for late-night relief beneath it. From the Counting House with its giant leather-bound ledgers and ceramic inkwells, you move to the Grinding House – a steam engine was used to power the circular grindstones, which lost their edge in no time at all. This is why you see so many retired grindstones everywhere, as treads of a stair or supporting an overhanging roof. What miserable, exhausting, back-breaking work it was though, labouring over a grindstone every day! What an angle you had to work at! From the Boring Shop you move to the Tilt Forge and then to the Crucible Furnace, with its five melting holes for the crucible pots, each one of which weighed 96 lbs. You needed muscle and back power in spades to be a Teemer. Over at the Hand Forge one of the resident blacksmiths – in eye-guard and beanie hat – is beating the hell out of a tongue of metal on a ringing anvil. 'You have to make 'em quick,' he says. 'It's all time and money.'

Address Abbeydale Road South, S7 2QW, +44 (0)114 272 2106, www.simt.co.uk/
abbeydale-industrial-hamlet, ask@simt.co.uk | Getting there Bus 97 or 98 from High Street
or Pinstone Street to attraction; or car: follow A 621 from city centre, on-site parking |
Hours Thu–Sat 10am–5pm Sun 11am–4pm | Tip Ladies Spring Wood, a delightful and
accessible snatch of ancient woodland, is visible on the hillside behind the hamlet.

2 Abbeydale Miniature Railway

Where delightful journeying never takes you far

We are all so in love with miniaturised worlds. The child reawakens within us to shocks of pleasure, often tinged with nostalgia. One of the most beguiling of these miniaturised worlds is in Abbeydale to the west of Sheffield, where a tiny steam rail network has been created by a team of enthusiastic railway model-makers – it's run by the Sheffield and District Society for Model and Experimental Engineers. Having walked up a path from a busy road, a gate welcomes you to the entire scene, which is played out against the backdrop of ancient woodland. It all feels quite rural and set apart, as if you have happened upon a delightfully sequestered country station (or two) in the middle of nowhere really. The tiny tracks travel in long ovals, one within another, returning you to within a few feet of where they set out. Such are the sizes of these trains that the driver, seated at the front, almost overwhelms the cab he sits in. The passengers travel behind in a single line, knees well tucked in, as the smoke gusts past and whistles blow lonesomely.

And then there is all the rest of the busy, clanky, day-to-day railway clutter to make everything happen: rolling stock with good solid brick sheds to shelter it from the elements; wooden bridges spanning the track; steam engines to tinker with; signalling apparatus; a tiny station named Abbeydale, complete with lovingly white-painted, stockade-style fencing and a protective canopy where you can stand, patiently waiting, just beyond reach of the elements. Bench-long lengths of track have been raised up for you to admire or walk between. And there's a *STOP* sign (when light flashes) beside the track on a wooden pole – white cross against black ground – beneath which we are instructed to *BEWARE OF TRAINS*. Of course.

Address Abbeydale Road South, S17 3LB, www.sheffieldmodelengineers.com | **Getting there** Bus 97 or 98 from High Street or Pinstone Street to near Amy's Ashram Hot Yoga Studio, opposite entrance to Ecclesall Woods; or car: follow A 621 from city centre and turn in to woods from opposite yoga studio | **Hours** Consult website for timetable | **Tip** Pass through a gate at the back of the enclosure, and you will find yourself in ancient Ecclesall Woods and a short way from a heronry.

3 Alfred Denny Museum

The fluorescent glow of Chaetopterus variopedatus

The Alfred Denny Museum of Zoology at the University of Shef-field, named after the university's first professor of biology, is a small, magically odd jewel of a place. This was once the zoology depart-ment's materials store. Here you can stare at a real specimen of, for example, the skeleton of a tiny pterodactyl. Or the skeleton of a porpoise, brought back on a bus from Sheffield's fish market in the 1950s. Nature's eye-delighting oddities are everywhere: the pouch of an opossum; a sea spider; a scorpion. Invertebrates (such as sponges) are displayed around the walls. Vertebrates – seal, hedge-hog, red squirrel, bat – are in the old wooden central cabinets, so finely made and so sturdy, which seem to process in a stately man-ner up the middle of the room. Drawers open to reveal collections of birds' eggs. The eye can scarcely credit how small and exquisitely formed the skulls of birds – great tit, red grouse, carrion crow – can be. The gold crest's is no bigger than a pea. One man brought all these tiny skulls in one day, in a couple of World War I suitcases, and offered them to the museum. No one thought to ask him where he'd got them from – or who he happened to be. Later, they felt a bit horrified that someone had created such an extraordinary col-lection of tiny skulls…

But perhaps the most exquisite part of the museum is the back-lit display of slides of marine organisms created by Henry Sorby, one of Sheffield's greatest scientists, and sometime correspondent of Charles Darwin. How did Sorby manage to squeeze and then seal all these specimens between two sheets of glass? How did this fan worm, for example, keep its shape? With the aid of a needle? They look like 35-mm slides, but in fact they are all real animals, and they look as fresh as on the day that they were mounted, at least 125 years ago.

Address The Alfred Denny Building, University of Sheffield, Western Bank, S10 2TN, +44 (0)114 222 2000, www.sheffield.ac.uk/alfred-denny-museum, animal.plant@sheffield.ac.uk | Getting there Bus 51, 52 or 52a from High Street to Western Bank; tram to University of Sheffield; or car: take A57 (Glossop), Q Park Durham Road car park | Hours First Sat of each month for guided tours at 10am, 11am and noon; booking essential | Tip A plaque set into the pavement tells you that the suffragette Adela Pankhurst once lived at 45 Marlborough Road, 15 minutes' walk from here.

4 Armandos Scooters

Vintage Lambrettas and Vespas posing like starlets

They are all lined up in front of the shop counter, handlebars turned provocatively side-on, a quartet of vintage Vespas and Lambrettas from the 1950s and 1960s, as sleek and as pretty in their lovely pastel greens and creams and greys as any bunch of starlets. These waspy-sounding machines are models of the ones Paul Newman and Audrey Hepburn posed on for publicity shots, so light, so zippy, so sensual. The earliest – the first were manufactured in 1946 – were only 98cc, and they were painted khaki because that was the only colour you could get at war's end.

Guido shows us some photographs in an old manual. The design has changed surprisingly little. He and his brother Giulio have been selling scooters from here for 40 years. Their father Armando, who trained as a mechanic in Milan, started the business back in the late 50s. The family comes from Oria, a medieval town in Puglia, deep in the south of Italy, that homeland of sweet tomatoes and olive oil, but Armando liked the idea of Sheffield because it was an industrial city. All the manuals were in Italian back then, so Armando translated them and started his own scooter shop. The boys grew up in the business.

The workshop which unfolds behind the counter is a wonderful maze of hanging spares – side panels, brake grips, helmets, clutch nuts, gear-oil-gleaming engines – and, of course, scooters needing urgent attention, one of which is hoisted up to eye level. Guido, who has grease beneath his fingernails, guides us through it all with the eye of an expert. If you drive around on one of these in Rome or Milan, he tells us, throwing his leg across one, everybody looks at you. This unique little Sheffield business gets enquiries from all over the world, but Guido, broad Sheffield accent notwithstanding, is still back in Puglia at heart. He goes there once a month. Armando, now retired, is already there.

Address Randall Street, S2 4SJ, +44 (0)114 273 0464, www.armandosscooters.com, sales@armandosscooters.com | Getting there Bus 75, 76, 97 or 98 from High Street or Pinstone Street to London Road/Hill Street, then walk down Hill Street to Randall Street, third on left; or car: Randall Street is just off Bramall Lane (A 621), on-street parking | Hours Wed–Fri 9am–4pm, Sat 9am–1pm | Tip Five minutes' walk from here, at 178–184 London Road, is Ozmen's International Food Centre, where you can pick up your Roasted Lemon Pistachios from Iran or Yum Yum Noodles from Thailand.

5 __ The Arctic Monkeys Room

Where the school kids from High Green practised

Andy pushes back the door of the recording studio, one of several in Yellow Arch Studios. He and his partner have been renovating and enlarging this Victorian factory with its cobbled courtyard for more than 15 years. They used to make giant nuts and bolts here. One fist-sized nut is still in use, as a hefty doorstop. 'This is the one they always want to see, the kids who come,' Andy says, opening the door. 'We call this one the Arctic Monkeys Room because this is where it all happened.'

The room itself isn't a fancy place at all – black sofa, chair, a table; walls cork-soundproofed (the sound proofing is a bit ripped); a bicycle hanging off the wall halfway up; a portrait of Elvis a bit higher up still, looking down like some rock deity keeping an eye on things; a hefty Marshall amp; ratty maroon carpeting; whitewashed brick walls; open fireplace. It is big though. In fact it is cavernous, with very tall ceilings. Andy agrees, with a vigorous nod. 'A room as cavernous as this one makes you sound good even if you're not,' he says, laughing. 'These kids *were* good though,' he quickly adds, 'don't get me wrong, but it took a lot of dedication, a lot of hard work. They used to drop in after school, most days, every tea time. They kept all their equipment here too.' Andy gestures to one far corner. 'They were about fourteen when their mums first dropped them off here after school, just four ordinary working-class kids from High Green with a consuming passion for guitar thrashing.'

Andy smiles and shakes his head as he thinks back. 'We did everything for them. We fed them. My wife taught Alex how to sing, and this is where they did it, recorded that first album. Then they left.'

You leave the studios by the old factory's cobbled courtyard. There's a yellow horseshoe over the arch – for good luck. The Arctic Monkeys certainly got lucky here.

Address 30–36 Burton Road, S3 8BX, +44 (0)114 273 0800, www.yellowarch.com, mail@yellowarch.com | **Getting there** Bus 7, 8 or 8a from Arundel Gate to Mowbray Street/Neepsend Lane, then cross road and walk up Ball Street to Burton Road; or car: from A 61 ring road, take B 6074, on-street parking nearby | **Hours** Thu & Fri 8.30am–4.30pm, Sat noon–2am, Sun noon–6pm, phone ahead to see the Arctic Monkeys Room | **Tip** The Milestone nearby on Kelham Island is a lovely Victorian gastropub.

6 The Bear Pit

Where Victorian roisterers threw buns

The three glass pavilions of Sheffield's Botanical Gardens, fronted by a sweep of smoothly manicured lawns punctuated by trees and raised flower beds, face down the Porter Valley with a pleasing degree of neoclassical composure. These gardens, recently restored, opened in 1836, just before the 19-year-old Queen Victoria ascended to the throne. Inside, the display of exotic shrubs and trees is themed by continent: in one, for example, there is an aspidistra plant, once fresh boated in from Asia, whose tough, leathery leaves seem so well suited to many a gloomy, overstuffed Victorian parlour. The *Graptopetalum paraguayense* from South America rises up like a gentle, multi-stemmed tooth flosser. Bad throat this morning? You will find that the Madagascar periwinkle is a medicinal cure-all. Matters turn sinister as we descend towards a spot hidden by dense trees and shrubs.

We come upon it all of a sudden, announced by a parapet of green railings, a stone-walled, circular pit which seems to plunge and plunge. The odd fern clings to its walls. Having descended a twisty track, we walk through an arched entrance way and then pad across tree bark – the metal gates slide closed behind us – to be greeted by a rearing, snub-snouted, jug-eared, cartoonish metal bear of over two metres in height. Tap it and it rings. Why a bear? This was once a bear pit. Bears were baited here, to the likely roar of onlookers from above. A regiment of troops, fresh back from the Crimean War in 1856, were entertained by a couple of bears in this pit after dining on roast beef and plum pudding. Children would throw buns and chunks of bread at them. This fun went on for about 30 years until the day when a nurse is said to have dangled a baby over the parapet and perhaps let it go. The bears feasted. Nowadays mums with strollers laugh at a rampant bear without an appetite.

Address Clarkehouse Road, S10 2LN, www.sbg.org.uk | **Getting there** 30-minute walk south-west of city centre; bus 81, 82, 83, 83a or 88 from Leopold Street to KFC on Ecclesall Road, then cross road and walk up Thompson Road to entrance; or car: take A 57 (Glossop), follow signs for Botanical Gardens, on-street parking around Clarkehouse Road | **Hours** Consult website for seasonal opening times | **Tip** Within five minutes' walk of the entrance to the garden on Clarkehouse Road is the church of St Mark's Broomhill, with a fine stained-glass west window by John Piper.

7__ Birdhouse Tea Company

The musical art of tea blending in Sidney Street

Julie English remembers very well how her daughter Becky, at the age of 13, developed a passion for the various tastes and aromas of loose-leaf teas. They were sitting in a small, street-corner cafe in Soho, London. Becky ordered green tea with jasmine blossoms. She was smitten. That was in 2001.

Now, almost two decades later, Becky is the expert when it comes to blending new varieties of tea at Birdhouse Tea Bar & Kitchen in Sidney Street at the heart of the Sheffield Cultural Industries Quarter. The business is a combination of a sunlit upstairs cafe which occasionally hosts a secret supper club, and a downstairs courtyard with a shop-front space. You can take your pick from individually packaged varieties of teas, all ranged in rows, a certain amount of coffee, and various essential tea accessories: tea pots, tea cups, infusor baskets, and, oh yes, good quality chocolate too - certain teas and chocolates, when taken in the mouth simultaneously, can release very particular flavours, Julie says.

Tea blending goes hand in hand with interesting phrases. Becky is after teas with particular tasting notes, her mother explains, as if tea blending were musical. Becky stands behind the counter, bashfully smiling. Their ambition is to blend unique, single-origin teas. Tea bags are flavourless by comparison because tea chopped up too finely loses its goodness. What exactly goes into these teas? Herbs, spices, fruits, oils, petals, cocoa bean husks.

Many of the names of the teas relate to Sheffield and the Peak District and their aroma is calculated to evoke a sense of place. Coles Corner, that meeting place for lovers at the city centre, is a tea made from jasmine green tea, dried fruit and rose petals. There are themed teas: wedding breakfast tea smells like wedding cake. Into the sweet-shop tea goes aniseed and liquorice.

Be infusiastic about tea! a sign reads.

Address Alsop Fields, Sidney Street, S1 4RG, +44 (0)114 327 3695, www.birdhouseteacompany.com, hello@birdshouseteacompany.com | Getting there 10-minute walk from Sheffield Station | Hours Mon – Fri 8.30am – 4.30pm, Sat & Sun 9am – 5pm | Tip Some of Sheffield's best graffiti artists work in the surrounding streets.

8 Bishop's House

The solid built yeoman's pad

Sheffield has an abundance of public parks, and each one is a mettlesome and unpredictable individualist. They canter on the flat for a stretch (perhaps keeping pace with a stream), plunge into a mysterious ravine or two, disappear into a dark coppice of trees, rise of a sudden up a steep incline, or take a mighty swerve to left or right as if in pursuit of some phantom beast.

Meersbrook Park is no exception to this gang of topographical oddities. It is top-and-tailed by two fine houses. Down in the valley's bottom is Meersbrook Hall, long home to the Ruskin Museum (see ch. 74). Then begins a long, steep, uphill climb, noting in passing the marvelous walled garden inside which you can enjoy the Museum of Gardening Tools, ably looked after by Kaktus (see ch. 53). At the top of the hill, only a little out of puff, you will spot Bishop's House, the best and most complete half-timbered building that Sheffield has to offer. It calls itself a bishop's house, but it does not quite have the size, the swagger or the pretentiousness that would befit any bishop. Instead it is a solid built piece of work, more appropriate to the kind of yeoman that would once have lived in it. These days, it is both a small museum of objects of the sort that might once have been inside the house, and a building for use in many different ways by the locals. On a Saturday night, for example, you might be sitting downstairs listening to a local rock/blues band consisting of 12-string guitar, blues harmonica and mandolin knocking out the tunes that have served them so well since Bob Dylan first came to this city in the 1960s and made it his home in spirit ever since.

Or perhaps – best of all – you will be able to enjoy a feature of the house that went on a walkabout for 150 years and was finally discovered during lockdown: the great oak fireplace in the parlour.

Address Norton Lees Lane, Meersbrook, Sheffield, S8 9BE, + 44 (0)114 255 7701, www.bishopshouse.org.uk | **Getting there** Bus 43, 44 or X17 from city centre to Beeton Road, right onto Brook Road, and 200 metres to park entrance; by car, take A61 (Heeley), turn left at Beeton Road, right onto Brook Road | **Hours** Sat & Sun 10am–4pm | **Tip** It's only a 10-minute walk from the bottom of the park to Abbeydale Road and its fine selection of junk shops.

9 Bobby's Lock-Up
Surveillance at a slower pace

Long before the police force of Sheffield could call on CCTV cameras, Rapid Response Units, Tasers, Smartphones or other zappy paraphernalia, there was this: on some strategic city street corner or other, a modest, box-like shed now painted green, topped by a glowing blue sign, which in its overall cosiness, smallness and even touching vulnerability, seems to resemble the kind of structure you might find down at the allotment, just next to the cabbages.

The City of Sheffield had 120 of these boxes from the 1930s onward, and this is the only one to survive into the present, tucked into one corner of Sheffield's rather grandiose Victorian Town Hall on Surrey Street, as if to poke a bit of fun at the relative scale of built structures.

You will see that it has a door, solid and well crafted, which lets you into a room almost too small to swing a kitten in. What exactly went on in this room? Well, messages – perhaps urgent ones – could be left by one bobby for the next. Or phoned through. *Help! Come soon! The city is ablaze.* That sort of thing. Or a bit of snap (Sheffieldish for food) could be had. Or it could even be used to lock up a criminal until such time as he could be carted off, perhaps in handcuffs, to a place more robust. The windows, you will notice, contain frosted glass – god forbid that the general public should ever see in. Notice how narrow the door seems to be – a reminder, perhaps, that human beings were more dapper, more whippet-like in shape, before fast foods made balloons of far too many of us. There is also a panel where a telephone would once have been, with the helpful message: *DIAL 0 FOR ASSISTANCE.*

These lovely boxes were the brainchild of Sheffield Chief Constable Percy J. Sillitoe, who had them installed in 1928. His next stint involved sorting out the unruly in Glasgow, where the very first boxes had been installed.

Address Surrey Street, adjacent to Town Hall, S1 2LG | **Getting there** 10-minute walk from bus and train station; buses through city centre stop nearby; tram to Cathedral; or car: Q Park Charles Street car park | **Hours** Unrestricted | **Tip** At the front of the Town Hall you will see a constellation of metal discs at your feet. These discs name some of the legends of Sheffield: Michael Palin, Gordon Banks, Sean Bean, Margaret Drabble and others.

10___Boot's Folly

A lonely tower in a wind-scoured field

If the lonely, high, wind- and rainswept land overlooking the Strines Reservoir to the west of Sheffield is the best place to look for UFOs – and there are said to have been strange sightings in these parts – the top of this building might have been the best vantage point from which to spot them. Not any more though. Now Boot's Folly, in all its handsome isolation, marooned three-quarters of the way down a field, is a ruin, and you venture in at your own risk. The main door that would once have shut out the world is gone, and the threshold has been rendered suckily boggy by cows' feet churning cow pats. The four enclosing walls remain, built from the stones of demolished properties, but the most likely visitor these days will be a cow or a rabbit. The stone-mullioned windows on all four sides could at first glance be 16th century. They are unglazed now, and the tower's upper floor disappeared long ago, though you can still see the pretty remnant of a winding staircase high above your gaze, ascending now to precisely nowhere. Nor is this place, proudly positioned on this eminence, even ancient, though it looks like a remnant of something old and significant.

Charles Boot, a prosperous local builder who lived in the nearby Sugworth Hall, built this folly in 1927. Castellated, and with a flagless flagpole, it resembles the tower of a castle, a fragment of something much greater and grander than itself. It is said by some that he built it this high – it rises to 315 metres – in order that he could see the tower of the parish church of High Bradfield, where his wife had been laid to rest.

When you reach it, you find nothing but walls, wind-filled spaces and perhaps the foetally curled carcase of a small animal amongst all the rubble, straw and cow reek. There are no plaques to be seen, and no explanations. If cows wander up, they are as taciturn as they come.

Address Bradfield Dale, South Yorkshire. According to Natural England, the landowner has granted permissive access because Boot's Folly is on the route of the Sheffield Country Walk, cwr.naturalengland.org.uk/mapboards/pdfs/AG00295982.pdf | Getting there By car: take the A 57 towards Manchester, past the South Yorkshire / Derbyshire border, then turn right at sign for Strines Inn, and right again half a mile later at sign for Bradfield and Ughill. After about a mile, you will find a set of locked gates and a sign announcing Sugworth Hall. Walk through footgate, and after 100 yards a footpath will direct you to the right, and through a rhododendron avenue around the back of the hall. Another footgate leads you into open land, and the folly. | Hours Unrestricted | Tip Just a short drive away is Strines Inn (www.thestrinesinn.webs.com), a dog-friendly 13th-century pub which does excellent food and has outside seating giving onto magnificent moorland.

11 Bragazzi's
Florentine deli with tractor stools

Matteo Bragazzi, wearing his knee-length, blue-and-white striped chef's apron, is sitting down for a moment, at a table near the window, just in front of three metal-bellied tractor stools. Those were the very first things he bought for his Italian deli, soon to be followed by every imaginable variety of Italian foodstuff, from the giant round of Parmigiano which sits on a shelf above our heads, to the pasta Peragallo from Genoa or the tiny tins of Leone peppermint pastels. He imports from all over Italy.

He opened here in Abbeydale in 2001, but his family, which comes from Massa Carrara in Tuscany – you can see photographs of his father and uncles on the walls – had been in the catering business since the early 1950s, in London. Central locations too: Frith Street, Rupert Street, the Haymarket. The trouble is that they did not adapt to changing times. They went on serving elaborate, multi-course meals when the world wanted something more informal. The kind of thing that you can find here.

In addition to the first-rate coffee, you can buy sandwiches in ciabbata or focaccia, all appealingly displayed in brimming wicker baskets on the counter, filled with whatever you might wish to choose from the list on the board or the cold cuts cabinet – roast pork loin with chargrilled artichoke, red or yellow pepper, and a herb and tomato marinade. There are other welcoming touches too – the day's newspapers are strewn about the tables. Matteo graduated in product design, and there is a designer's eye at work here, everywhere – in the abstract patterning of the gleaming copper piping above our heads, for example, or the tiling on the walls. Unusual eye-catching objects hang from the ceiling: a red fly swat, a yellow dustpan. Why did he decide to open this place? He had a whimsical bet with his mother, in Rome. She said he wouldn't. He did.

Plain Focaccia

Fontina
Mortadella
Rocket Pesto
Vine Tomato

£4.20

Address 224 Abbeydale Road, S7 1FL, +44 (0)114 258 1483, www.bragazzis.co.uk, info@bragazzis.co.uk | Getting there Bus 97 or 98 from Sheffield Interchange to the stop after Chippinghouse Road; or car: take the A621 to Abbeydale Road, on-street parking | Hours Mon – Sat 9am – 4.30pm | Tip The Broadfield Ale House, one of Sheffield's finest pubs and a purveyor of excellent meat pies, is within an easy walk of here at 452 Abbeydale Road. Turn right out of Bragazzi's and keep going for about five minutes.

12 The Buffer Girls

At the filthy end of the metalworking process

The buffer girls of Sheffield, generally toiling in rows, were at the filthy end of the metalworking process. It was their job to stand in front of a spinning wheel of leather or cloth lubricated with a mixture of oil and sand, and hold the blade or other metal object to it until it shone temptingly smooth, bright-polished, shop-counter-ready. They wore unlovely headscarves and neckerchiefs and their legs were swathed in brown parcel paper held in place by string. The sleeves of their garments were short, as there could be few things more dangerous than getting clothing caught in fast-moving machinery.

These two, teenagers when they posed for this painting, were called Maggie Herrick (right) and Jane Gill (left), and they worked for Walker & Hall, specialists in silver, electroplate and Britanniaware metal goods on Howard Street, which is less than a five-minute walk from where the painting is currently on display in the Sykes Gallery Metalwork Collection. The painter, Sir William Rothenstein, a Bradford man, was in employment as Professor of Civic Art at Sheffield University when he made this painting. The girls – one stares directly at us; the other looks to the side – seem wearily dignified in demeanour, stoical, resigned, somewhat blank-eyed. The headscarves hold their hair in place, lumpishly.

Their tedious, noisy, smelly, shoulder-punishing world is evoked very vividly in *Granny Was a Buffer Girl*, the Carnegie Award-winning novel by Sheffield author Berlie Doherty, whose own grandmother had been a buffer girl. Granny Dorothy, we read, 'couldn't keep the smell of the buffing shop out of her clothes and her shoes and her hair. Her father had always hated that smell; and so did she.' Forty girls, heads averted from the sand and dust, breathed in that sickly-sweet smell of heat and metal all day long. Later they would swill their mouths out with tap water.

Address Sykes Gallery: Metalwork Collection, Millennium Gallery, Arundel Gate, S1 2PP, +44 (0)114 278 2600, www.museums-sheffield.org.uk, info@museum-sheffield.org.uk | Getting there Enter via Arundel Gate or through The Winter Garden on Surrey Street | Hours Tue–Sat 10am–5pm, Sun 11am–4pm, Mon, Sheffield school holidays and Bank Holidays 10am–5pm | Tip A full-height mannequin of a Buffer Girl at work is in the Kelham Island Museum, dressed for all her dirty, exhausting toil.

13___The Cementation Furnace

At the birth of global steel-making

Hemmed in by a car park these days, which is itself surrounded by old manufacturing buildings long under threat of demolition, and impregnated by a steady, low roar from major arterial roads, this shapely, conical, red-brick structure – it looks like a pregnant, upturned egg cup with a flourish of a chimney on top – is the sole survivor of what were once hundreds in this city of a steel-making process first developed in the early 17th century, more than 200 years before Henry Bessemer created his celebrated convertor. It is a rare remnant of the oldest steel-making technology in the world. Sprigs of hardy weed are growing out from between the mortar-thirsty bricks of its swelling walls. Two additional straight brick walls hold it steady. You can see somewhat into the heart of it from the back.

How did it work? Steel-making was a matter of combining iron with charcoal in the right proportions. Bars of imported wrought iron were packed into stone chests or coffins sealed off from the air by a mixture of sludge and dust. It was then raised, slowly, to a red (never molten) heat by a fire burning in a grate beneath, which kept it at a constant temperature for more than a week. The iron's slow absorption of the charcoal brought into being a marvellous new product called steel. When cool enough, workers climbed in and broke through the surface of what was known as 'wheelswarf'. The finished product had an unlovely, bubbly surface, hence its name: blister steel. There are words associated with the creation of blister steel which have seeped into the local dialect. After heating, the steel's 'pie-crust' turned rock-hard. That rock-hard surface was known as crozzle, and the onomatopoeically characterful adjective 'crozzled' is still used by Sheffielders to describe over-cooked chips – or perhaps a fiercely over-grilled cheese topping.

Listen out for it at your local chippie.

Address Doncaster Street, S3 | **Getting there** Bus 81, 82, 85 or 86 from Arundel Gate to Shalesmoor, then walk up Shepherd Street and right into Doncaster Street; tram to Shalesmoor, then walk up Hoyle Street and along Doncaster Street; or car: access from A61 (Barnsley) via Hoyle Street and Doncaster Street, on-street parking nearby | **Tip** Ten minutes' walk from here is the Nichols Building – a right turn off the Shalesmoor roundabout – an old factory full of vintage clothes, furniture, crockery and other collectibles.

14__The Central Library

Sheffield's street-corner, Art Deco fanfare

Sheffield's Central Library is the city's Art Deco masterpiece, and it remains, inside and out, much as it was when it first opened. The product of a meticulous collaboration between W. G. Davies, the City Architect, and J. P. Lamb, the Chief Librarian, it was erected by men from the Direct Labour Department of Sheffield Corporation. Lamb made detailed drawings of all the library's furnishings, and you recognise the harmonious and dignified continuity of its crafting in things large and small, from door handles to air vents and metalwork screens. The total cost? £148,211.

It was a species of visionary enthusiasm that brought into being the great public libraries of Sheffield from the second half of the 19th century onwards. Books could be tools of enlightenment and self-betterment, in the opinion of such local lobbyists for the cause as Richard Gilly the iron-master and William Fisher the Younger, who traded in horn and ivory. And in 1934, the greatest lending library of them all was created. The building also houses a small theatre and the Graves Art Gallery (see ch. 37).

The chief wood used was oak, with walnut inlay. The chairs you can sit in – heavy, solid, comfortable, dependably supportive – when you visit the Local Studies' Library, are the same chairs you would have sat in on opening day. They have been polished to near perfection over 80 years of continuous bum-and-back buffering. Especially pleasing are the recessive oak door surrounds, which remind you a little of entering into the pleasures of reading a book. There is an air of the fanciful about some of the details of the exterior. The building's corner onto Tudor Square seems to thrust it forward at an angle, presenting us with a balcony that might have been borrowed from some Venetian palazzo and then, high above, Egypt, in the figure of Knowledge, squats on the world.

Address Surrey Street, S1 1XZ, +44 (0)114 273 4712 | **Getting there** Buses passing through city centre stop close by; tram to Castle Square; or car: Q Park Charles Street car park | **Hours** Mon, Tue, Thu, Fri 10am–5pm, Wed 10am–8pm | **Tip** The *Women of Steel* statue in Barker's Pool two minutes away commemorates local female steel workers of the First and Second World Wars.

15__Chantrey's Needle

The greatest portrait sculptor of his age

Chantrey's great granite obelisk, 22 feet in height, with its triple-stepped plinth, now sits, austere and self-vaunting, at a casual bend of the road beside the village green, metres in front of the railinged, yew-tree-shaded family vault in the churchyard of St James the Great, the parish church of the Sheffield suburb of Norton.

It was designed by Chantrey's long-time friend Philip Hardwick, RA. Like all such obelisks, it is very simple and very plain, and the inscription is as bald and brief as they come: *Chantrey*, it reads. Chantrey. A mellifluous name indeed. Like the ring of a bell. That's all though. No dates. Why more anyway? Because those who erected it – it was paid for by public subscription – would have said to themselves that only a fool would be unaware of the status and the achievements of this Sheffield man, Sir Francis Chantrey, the greatest portrait sculptor of his age. The people of London had wanted him to be interred in Westminster Abbey, but a note written by Chantrey had insisted otherwise. His wish was to be buried in the churchyard he had known as a child, and his wish prevailed. The body was transported back – hearse, mourning coach (each pulled by a team of four horses), and preceded by four additional horsemen – all the way from where he had died in London. And had there not been hundreds at his burial in 1841 to commemorate the man who had been commissioned to sculpt the portrait bust of His Majesty King George III?

He had grown up local and quite poor. Born in 1781, as a child he had delivered milk by donkey. Later the young Chantrey, still eking out a meagre living, had done portrait commissions for two to three guineas apiece. Then he went to London, and became good friends with Sir Benjamin West, president of the young Royal Academy of Arts. Clients came flocking: clerics, aristocrats, painters. He became an eminence.

Address Norton Lane, S8 | Getting there Bus 1 or 1a from High Street or Pinstone Street to Norton Lane, across road from Norton Church; or car: take A 61 (Chesterfield) then A 6102 to Norton Lane, on-street parking | Tip Sheffield Cathedral houses a portrait bust of Rev James Wilkinson, Chantrey's first work in marble.

16 Cresswell Crags

It was 27,000 years ago today…

The only examples of Ice Age rock art ever to be discovered in the United Kingdom are engraved on the walls and the ceiling of a dank, dark place called Church Hole Cave within a limestone gorge a short drive south-east of Sheffield. Cresswell Crags, two towering flanks of craggy, compacted, tree-smothered limestone 260 million years of age, which face each other like a pair of dangerously tetchy rivals, are kept apart by a long boating pond created by the Duke of Portland in the 1860s. The rock was so soft that water cut through it to create the caves that we can see to this day. Who ever thought that soft rock couldn't look like Swiss cheese?

The Discovery Centre, tucked well out of sight of the ancient gorge itself, shows off samples of what has been found in these caves ever since the Victorians got to work with their pickaxes and their dynamite, destroying just as much as they preserved. Sprawled on its belly like a newborn babe in a hospital incubator is the complete skeleton of a baby hyena. That species would have been roaming these parts 40,000 years ago. You can peer down and count the rib bones. It was discovered in 1980 in Pin Hole Cave.

After a short walk up beside the lake, you come to the foot of the entrance to one or another of the cave mouths, part-disguised by trees, closed to trespassers by metal gates. The hidden caves in these rocky flanks have names like Mother Grundy's Parlour and Robin Hood Cave, and are reached by climbing long flights of wooden stairs that ascend into the dark. You wear a hard white hat for protection, with a light that packs a powerful beam. Inside, you pick your way across slippery, uneven ground, banging your hat a time or two against the swooping and diving ceiling, and then finger one of the stone tools that would have been found here. The first humans preceded you here by about 27,000 years.

Address Crags Road, Creswell, Worksop, S80 3LH, +44 (0)1909 720378,
www.creswell-crags.org.uk | Getting there By car: take A 57 or A 60, then B 6042, parking
outside the Discovery Centre | Hours Consult website | Tip And now for a Michelangelo?
The Harley Gallery on the Welbeck Estate is five minutes' drive from here.

17__Cubana

Bringing over those Latino dance rhythms

Where do you go to find the sights, tastes and rhythms of Latin America in Sheffield? Cubana is deep inside a courtyard square in the city centre, and as soon as you enter, you begin to imbibe its hip-swaying, foot-tapping spirit – and that is not an indirect reference to the range of rums on offer behind the bar on the ground floor, which is second only, in range and quality, to what you would find in London (the best and the most expensive costs £150 a shot). The driving Latino music, all those rasping trumpets, escort you in by the arm. There are murals and paintings on the walls: a street scene from old Havana; portraits of the Buena Vista Social Club blowing on their horns. Che Guevara puffs serenely on a cigar at the head of the staircase that takes you to the upstairs restaurant. The serious dancing goes on in the sultry, dim-lit downstairs, usually to a live band. Salsa classes happen down here too, just beside the long bar, which is overlooked by images of Che and Jesus. Behind you, in a trompe l'oeil painting, a shutter has been thrown back onto a sun-struck square.

This restaurant is the creation of Adrian Bagnoli, a son of Italian immigrants from the 1950s. His father wanted a job in the steelworks. Adrian, never a great achiever at school, eventually became a pen-pushing civil servant, but his life changed 25 years ago when he took a year-long sabbatical on cruise ships which transported him to Latin America. How they danced over there! Not grimly smoochy as in Sheffield, but with a kind of smiley, energetic vitality. Couldn't he bring this back to Sheffield? He did. The food – hot tapas – is Latin American laced with Spanish: *cordero in vino tinto, cerdo y calabacin…* Buena Vista Social Club have visited the place, as has Che's daughter. The chief chef is Chilean, and the rest of the workforce is Latino too. Let's dance, baby.

Address Unit 4, Leopold Street, S1 2JG, +44 (0)276 0475, www.cubanatapasbar.co.uk |
Getting there 2-minute walk from Town Hall | Hours Mon–Wed noon–2am, Thu
12.30pm–1am, Fri 12.30pm–1am, Sat noon–3am, Sun 1pm–midnight | Tip Ten minutes'
walk from here is the Moore Street Electricity Substation, one of Sheffield's greatest
brutalist buildings.

18__ The Curzon Cinema
Complete with tour of the bank vaults

The Curzon, Sheffield, is not a typical place. This is a bijou, luxury cinema with a difference: high projection sound, reclining seats, and programming which ranges from the cult to the indie, taking in a snatch of Hollywood too. Its three intimate auditoria – which seat 35, 55 and 65, respectively – resemble three carefully sculpted, carefully positioned boxes, and are neatly, and quite self-sufficiently, located inside a listed building which first opened its doors as the George Street Tea Room in 1788, and morphed into a bank in 1873. The recreational areas – long corridors with plenty of comfortable chairs and tables to choose from; arched, street-facing windows – are spacious and plentiful.

Did you hear the word bank? Yes, and this is why your Curzon, Sheffield experience could turn a mite surreal. Today's cinema visit could also include a visit to the bank vaults – if, that is, you remember to book it in advance. The old vaults are directly underneath the vestibule where you were perhaps expecting to do little other than buy your tickets. Who could refuse though? Down the stairs you go, into a forbiddingly atmospheric basement, complete with steely-grey floors, cell-like rooms barred off in the style of any county sheriff's lock-up, massively reinforced iron doors inches thick and, a little surprisingly, the cinema's spanking new high-tech projection room, full of banks of computers kept at a constant, cooling 17 degrees centigrade. Occasionally you encounter chilling signage from the recent past: *Caution: before locking up strong rooms, key holder must make certain that no one is left inside.* Is that a smell of decay? Surely not. Look out for the chain-pull lift which carried the money up and down before you make your way back up to the newly reassuring life of leisure time well spent in the present moment.

Is *The Hatton Garden Job* showing upstairs?

Address 16 George Street, S1 2PF, +44 (0)1223 555644, www.curzoncinemas.com/sheffield/info | **Getting there** Tram to Castle Square; car park: NCP Arundel Gate | **Hours** Tours of the bank vault need to be organised in advance | **Tip** In the window of Bar 1857 opposite, you will find a display in celebration of Sheffield FC, founded in 1857, the world's oldest football club.

19 _ The Cutlers' Hall

Where masters of industry strutted their stuff

If Sheffield were ever to have the equivalent of a king (and god forbid that such a hotbed of socialist dissent should ever countenance such a thing), and if the splendour and outrageous panache of the Cutlers' Hall is anything to go by, that title would sit well on the shoulders of the Master Cutler of Hallamshire. The name of Sheffield has been synonymous with the making of cutlery since at least the 14th century – did not the poet Geoffrey Chaucer refer, rather chillingly, to the Reeve's Sheffield knife, hidden in his hose, in *The Canterbury Tales*? This is the place from which the cutlery trade has been regulated since the 17th century, though the building which now stands on this site is a 19th-century creation. So many full-length portraits of the great industrial fabricators of Sheffield are on display here in its sweeping staterooms, which are approached up a pompous double staircase, watched over by an early portrait of Her Majesty the Queen. Above that staircase hangs one of the greatest curios of this institution: a giant circular electrolier (a hanging chandelier whose lights are powered by electricity) of metal and stained glass dating from 1936, whose battery of lights help to illuminate a brilliant glass panel blazing forth the Sheffield Coat of Arms. Look out for the crossed swords, the arrows, the sheaves of hay and, circling that central panel, the parade of elephant heads, reminding us of the use of ivory in the making of knife handles.

To find an even more handsome electrolier, you need to proceed to the 1832 wing, where you will spot a lovely, brooch-like, oval specimen, quite as good as any to be seen on the *Lusitania* or the doomed *Titanic*, scavenged from the *RMS Olympic* by Thomas Ward of Sheffield in 1936, who had been given the task of breaking up the ship and disposing of anything of value.

Don't miss the display cases bristling with Sheffield knives.

Address Church Street, S1 1HG, +44 (0)114 276 8149, www.cutlershall.co.uk | Getting there City centre, directly opposite the cathedral | Hours Telephone ahead to book a tour | Tip Almost opposite the hall, hidden amongst trees in the cathedral grounds, is a statue of the great dissenter and hymn-writer, James Montgomery.

20___The Cutting Edge
A sculptural greeting in steel and water

If it's the train that spirits you into Sheffield Station, a surprising sight will meets your eyes as you descend the stairs to the station forecourt. Through the plate-glass windows which face into Sheaf Square, your eyes will bounce off a curving, shimmering wall of rearing steel which seems to be snaking away from you uphill in a processional fashion, and, just to its left, a series of weirs down which water rushes, culminating in the fist-like gush of a fountain.

Sheffield greets you with this spectacle of water and shaped steel together, two of this city's fundamental anchors and sources of prosperity. You will not easily find either a name for this sculpture or any reference to its maker. That too is characteristic. Sheffield is an unshowy-offy city with a powerful communal spirit, and this seems to be borne out in the pleasing anonymity of this work. As you approach, you see how it is being used and enjoyed by the public. Students take selfies against the iridescent wall of streaming, reflective water. Children play in it. Others press their hands against it, as if not quite knowing what this thing is. Only touch will make it come clear. And as the wall of steel rises up its gentle incline, it very subtly diminishes in height and changes in shape. At the bottom end it is a soaring, five-metre-high ellipse, down which the water streams. As it makes its snaking way uphill, it shrinks in height and increases in roundedness, so that by the time you reach its far end, it is not so much a pointed ellipse as a barrel. Both hollow ends are blocked off by panels of stained glass.

The sculpture is called *The Cutting Edge* – a near perfect summation of the spirit of the city it seems to represent, somewhat ethereally, in spite of its massiness – and it is a collaboration between Chris Knight, Brett Payne and Keith Tyssen of Si Applied of Sheffield, and the Japanese glass artist Keiko Mukaide.

Address Sheaf Square, S1 2LW | Getting there Buses through city centre to Interchange; tram to Sheffield Station / Hallam University; or car: Sheffield Station Q Park Turner Street car park | Hours Unrestricted | Tip As you walk up Howard Street towards the city centre, look up and right to admire 'What If?', a poem sited high on a wall of Sheffield Hallam University, written by Andrew Motion, a former Poet Laureate.

21 Dale Dyke Dam

The near hidden source of great tragedy

Dale Dyke Dam is just one of a necklace of public reservoirs that supply the drinking water of Sheffield. It is also a dam that provokes shudders of horror. One inclement night in March 1864, a crack opened up in this dam wall – it was earthen then, not stone as now – and 700 million gallons of water laid waste to everything downstream that lay in its path along the Loxley and Don Valleys – farms, mills, livestock, and more than 250 human beings. The Great Sheffield Flood was one of the greatest man-made disasters of the 19th century.

These days the dam is a much smaller and more low-key affair, and it's hidden away at the bottom of a track. The first you know of it is a fingerpost beside a road pointing down to a public footpath that begins at a breach in a wall at a low-scooping turn of the road. But where exactly is the water? This place doesn't shout about itself.

Having walked several hundred metres downhill, shouldering your way through bracken to the accompaniment of the roo-cooing of doves, crunching pine cones underfoot as you go, you finally come across a small, round-headed stone on which is inscribed a single mysterious word: *CLOB*. This is one of four stones marking the centre line of the dam's original bank. A plaque explains why we are here and, descending still further, having passed through a couple of kissing gates, the stone embankment wall of the dam itself hoves into view.

All is relatively peaceful today on the grey, breeze-diced water. A small flotilla of ducks warns us to keep our distance. A strew of bone-dry tree limbs litter the embankment wall. A conifer plantation rises up the hillside. There are mother-pestering lambs in the fields. At water's edge, almost hidden by foliage, a sobering sign in red lettering reminds us of this place's terrible past. *COLD WATER KILLS*, it reads. It does indeed.

Address Postcode S6 6LE, OS grid reference SK 245920 | Getting there Take bus 61 or 62 from city centre (Arundel Gate) or Hillsborough Interchange to Low Bradfield, alighting at turning circle at junction of Annet Lane / Fairhouse Lane. Walk down Annet Lane, then left down Blindside Lane. Roughly two-mile walk via public footpath on right down to reservoir. | Hours Unrestricted | Tip A sobering memorial to the dead of the flood from the Malin Bridge area is in St Polycarp's Church.

22 — The David Mellor Factory

Sitting pretty inside a gasometer's footprint

Why is the David Mellor Factory, with its sloping roof so reminiscent of the spokes of a bicycle wheel, circular? Because it sits on the footprint of an old gas works, and gasometers, when empty (there were two of them here), are great, hollow drums. Mellor, Sheffield's most innovative and celebrated post-war master metalworker, created this tiny cutlery factory with its outbuildings (the space where the gas was made now houses a library) towards the end of his life, both as a space to work and a space to live, and around it, thanks to the continuing efforts of his designer son Corin (the family still lives on-site), other buildings have continued to grow. There is now a handsome cafe tucked inside a small design museum which tells the story of Mellor's own evolution as a maker; a shop selling the work of Mellor and others – from knives and forks to egg cups, walnut trays and Finnish glass; the factory itself; and a display of Mellor's street furniture close to the car park, which disconcerts any driver fresh out of his vehicle. Why? Well, is not street furniture, even when designed by David Mellor – such objects as a postbox, a bus shelter which seems to set your location as Sloane Square in Chelsea when you believed yourself to be deep amidst the beauty of the Derbyshire hills, and, worst of all, a set of working traffic lights – there to demand obedience?

In the factory – which Corin, such are its dimensions, insists upon calling a workshop – Mellor cutlery is made, from start to finish. The entire enterprise consists of 35 people, and 27 of them toil inside this drum, which contains the intricate machinery, much old, some new, to enable you to custom-make a fork or a knife. A wall panel describes the 35 different processes an item of cutlery may need to go through before it sits, elegant and utile, in your hand, poised for action at the dinner table.

Address The Round Building, Hathersage, S32 BA, +44 (0)1433 650220,
www.davidmellordesign.com, davidmellor@davidmellordesign.co.uk | Getting there
Bus 271 or 272 from Sheffield Interchange to Hathersage village centre, then walk for about
15 minutes down the B6001 (towards Bakewell) and under railway bridge to factory on left;
train to Hathersage (Hope Valley Line); or car: take A625 from city centre to Hathersage,
then B6001, where you follow signs to on-site parking | Hours Mon–Sat 10am–5pm,
Sun 11am–5pm | Tip Hathersage has a delightful, heated, open-air swimming pool
(www.hathersageswimmingpool.co.uk).

23_Derek Dooley's Way

The bobby-dazzler with a foot in both camps

Football is always a fiercely partisan affair, and nowhere more so than in Sheffield, where you are either for the Owls (Sheffield Wednesday) or the Blades (Sheffield United). When a pigeon-fancier up on Skye Edge remarks that this is the best view in Sheffield, and gazes in a certain direction, you know that she is staring with loving loyalty at the terraces of Bramall Lane, Sheffield United's ground, which is clearly visible down in the valley. Yet Sheffield's greatest footballing hero managed – by a tragic miracle – to be an ecumenical figure who, by the end of his life, had served both clubs, and was revered by fans of both teams.

This man, a hero on the pitch to supporters of Sheffield Wednesday, where he was a formidably strong, swift-moving, goal-scoring centre forward in the early 1950s, and to Sheffield United too, where he served in later life, was the great, Sheffield-born Derek Dooley. Is the inner ring road called Derek Dooley Way because he ran rings around so many in his time?

Dooley played like a fast-moving bull. He was raw-boned, short on finesse, and strong on the sheer physical power required to bundle a man – even a goalkeeper – off a ball. Would some of those goals have been disallowed these days? Perhaps. Tragedy struck after an away match at Preston, when he was 23 years old, and in his prime as a player. He broke a leg. Gangrene set in. The leg was amputated. He later became manager of the club for two years, but he was eventually dismissed on Christmas Eve of 1973. He found a new career as commercial manager for Sheffield United, and, later, chairman of the board.

Dooley's statue stands in the executive car park at Bramall Lane, close to that of Joe Shaw, Sheffield United's greatest centre half, who was set down on this earth to outfox and frustrate the ambitions of the likes of a Dooley. Owls and Blades salute him without acrimony.

Address Bramall Lane, S2 4SU | Getting there Bus 252 from Sheffield Interchange to Sheffield United Football Ground, or 3, 3a, 43 or 44 (Chesterfield) or 252 from Arundel Gate; or car: from Sheffield Station, at the Sheaf Street roundabout continue ahead onto Suffolk Street and at the Granville Square roundabout, turn right onto St Mary's Road, taking the second left into Shoreham Street where the ground is on the right, on-site parking | Hours Unrestricted | Tip Hagglers Corner, a great place to have a coffee or listen to live music, is a short walk from here at 586 Queens Road.

24 Derwent Bridge

Rescued from drowning stone by stone

Sheffield is ringed by many reservoirs created to slake the thirst of those who once panted beside the hell mouths of the furnaces in the Don Valley. Three of the most beautiful – Ladybower, Derwent and Howden, all linked together like droplets on a neck chain – act as great, man-made containers for the waters of the Derwent Valley. They are giants. Derwent alone has a capacity of over two billion gallons. Mighty twin stone towers – akin to Florentine watchtowers – span the great embankments separating the dams. The valley's wooded slopes, coniferous and deciduous, rise to meet fields and swelling moorland. There are dribbles of sheep, and the occasional picturesquely ruinous fragment of drystone walling.

These reservoirs are haunted by human displacement because they are drowned valleys, and each silent body of water has its own arresting story to tell. As you travel beside the water, you'll spot stone footings of long vanished houses, once the temporary homes of the workers whose job it was to demolish the properties of the inhabitants of such villages as Derwent and Ashopton, which were cleared in 1943 and submerged to create the Ladybower Dam. It was over the waters of the Derwent Dam that the Lancaster Bombers of 617 Squadron flew, in their practice runs for the coming 'Dambusters' assault upon the Ruhr Valley in 1947. In 1954, filmmakers used this place as a location for The Dam Busters, in which the valley played not itself but doubled as the Ruhr Valley.

A 17th-century bridge from the village of Derwent survives to this day, having been transported stone by stone up valley, beyond the head of the Howden Reservoir, to a place called Slippery Stones. We know exactly where it would once have stood because of a 1925 painting by celebrated local artist Stanley Royle, which shows the bridge in the heart of the village, dappled by sunlight.

Address Slippery Stones, head of Howden Reservoir | **Getting there** Buses infrequent, so best by car: via the A 57 toward Glossop. Turn immediately right after crossing Ladybower Reservoir (signed Derwent Valley) to Fairholmes. Road from Fairholmes to King's Tree has variable opening times. Car park at Fairholmes or roadside parking at King's Tree. Twenty-minute walk from King's Tree to bridge. | **Hours** Unrestricted | **Tip** There is a lovely natural swimming hole a short distance upstream from the bridge.

25 — The Dore Stone

Where England became a political entity

The kingdom known as England first became a physical and administrative reality in the village of Dore, which is now one of Sheffield's prettiest western suburbs, and this remote outpost was then established as the northernmost boundary of that kingdom. The stone which marks what happened at this historic place sits at the top corner of the old village green, at the apex of a triangle of land bounded by old drystone walls, at the point where Savage Lane meets Vicarage Lane, just a stone's throw from a memorial to those who died in World Wars I and II. Over at the war memorial, the statue of a young soldier stands rigidly to attention. There are four simple wooden crosses at the statue's foot, and a few dishevelled poppies indicative of some fairly recent attention. All this serves as a reminder of relatively fresh spilled blood: the Sheffield City Battalion lost more than 500 men at the Battle of the Somme in 1916.

There is no reminder of human sacrifice at the Dore Stone because there was no bloodshed of any kind at that remoter date. The memorial itself is a smooth, pear-shaped plaque in the form of a Saxon shield, set into a rough-hewn, upright slab of stone, at one end of a somnolent pocket of green some way up a gently rising hillside. The words incised, picked out in gold, neatly tapering off beneath a rampant dragon, tell the story of that momentous occasion. There was no fighting when England was unified, merely an agreement between two rival kings to regard their twin territories as one. In fact, it was an act of extraordinary capitulation by one overlord to another, this momentous non-battle, and it happened approximately 1,300 years ago. Two armies came together on that day, King Eanred's from the northern kingdom of Northumbria, and King Ecgbert's from Wessex to the south. Eanred capitulated to Ecgbert in the year ad 829.

What a secret for a somnolent village green.

KING ECGBERT OF WESSEX
LED HIS ARMY TO DORE
IN THE YEAR A·D 829
AGAINST KING EANRED
OF NORTHUMBRIA
BY WHOSE
SUBMISSION
KING ECGBERT
BECAME FIRST
OVERLORD
OF ALL
ENGLAND

Address The Village Green, Dore, S17 3GW | **Getting there** Bus 81 from Leopold Street to Causeway Head Road, then a few minutes' walk; train to Dore and Totley, then walk up Dore Road; or car: approximately 1 mile from A625 near Dore Moor pub, turn onto Cross Lane and continue along Causeway Head Road, or, from A621, turn up Dore Road (opposite Dore and Totley station), on-street parking | **Hours** Unrestricted | **Tip** The very first Anglo-Saxon helmet to be excavated in England was found south-west of Sheffield, and its ruinous remains, together with a reconstruction, are on display in the city's Weston Park Museum.

26 Ecclesall Woods

Neolithic rock art in ancient woodlands

Sheffield is thronging with pockets of ancient woodland. There are 70 of them in all, occupying approximately 3,000 acres of land. They sidle up to estates of houses in Fir Vale, defying modernity to do its worst. They fling themselves along entire lengths of valleys – sample the hanging beech woods, with their fierce, tentacular, hillside-gripping, semi-exposed roots, which canopy the path through the Limb Valley up to Ringinglow. Ecclesall Woods to the west, criss-crossed by bridle paths, are amongst the largest. In fact, they are as big as 200 football pitches. These have always been working or 'coppice' woods, used by generations of families to gain meagre livings as makers of brooms, baskets or charcoal, and there is evidence of human endeavour, half hidden amongst the trees, everywhere. The most poignant record of human usage of all is the memorial, raised by acquaintances, in memory of George Yardley, an 18th-century charcoal maker who was *Burnt to death in his Cabbin* on 11 October, 1786.

These woods change and change again throughout the seasons – there are beds of bluebells in May, sweet chestnuts to be gathered or carelessly kicked aside by the little-knowing in late October. Never quite getting lost, you come upon marvels, repeatedly – a strange hollow in the shadow of a chestnut tree, for example, tells you that white coal has been worked for. Or have you found evidence of a charcoal hearth? Perhaps ask for advice from the J G Graves Discovery Centre. You could sign up for a course in woodland skills at the same time and make your own spatula. Best of all in these woods is the indisputable evidence that Neolithic man once made his rock art close to the centre of Sheffield. It is in a clearing on its own, a mossy stone, slightly bulbous, slightly sensual, with deep scorings round and across it. Archaeologists call these cup-and-ring markings.

Address Limb Lane, Dore, S17, grid reference SK 323 824, +44 (0)114 250 0500. For information about the exact whereabouts of the cup-and-ring stone, parksandcountryside@sheffield.gov.uk (Emails will not be responded to at weekends.) | **Getting there** Bus 97 or 98 from city centre to the junction of Abbey Lane, and then walk up; or car: take Abbeydale Road South (A 621), on-street parking off Limb Lane, Dore and adjoining Abbey Lane, or Whirlowdale Road | **Hours** Unrestricted | **Tip** The J G Graves Woodland Discovery Centre in Ecclesall Woods offers heritage craft courses all the year round.

27 Edward Carpenter

Gay activist and pioneering sandal-maker

The writer and pioneering gay-rights activist Edward Carpenter, one of Sheffield's many under-sung heroes, was born into an emotionally frigid, middle-class family in Brighton in 1844. Educated at Cambridge University, he travelled to Sheffield as a lecturer for the first time in 1877. What he discovered there changed his life forever. He had never met the kinds of people he encountered in the north of England. Though often lacking in formal education, they had a rude openness, a fearless curiosity, an attachment to nature, and a warmth that shocked and delighted him.

He was accepted for who he was. There was no high and no low. Having been welcomed into the bosom of a farmer's family in Bradway, he eventually settled, with his partner George Merrill, in a small cottage in Millthorpe, a village set in the Cordwell Valley between Sheffield and Chesterfield. What is more, he became an artisan, a passionate believer in the solid virtues of manual labour, whether it be market-gardening or the building of a wall. Surprisingly, and thanks to an unexpected gift from a well-wisher in India, he discovered that he also possessed a surprising talent for the making of sandals.

Carpenter's Sheffield story is, in part, the pursuit of a ghost. The Victorian Sheffield that he knew has vanished. The institute where he lectured is gone. Handsome young men no longer take part in naked running races down Fargate, as they once used to do much to Carpenter's delectation. What remains are Carpenter's papers and some of his belongings, which are kept at the Sheffield Archives. These belongings include two pairs of his sandals, hand-crafted by him at Millthorpe in the 1890s. Carpenter believed in bodily liberation. He regarded the boot as the coffin of the foot. His sandals were eagerly commissioned by those whose feet needed liberating from bunions and other pedestrian torments.

Address Sheffield Archives, 52 Shoreham Street, S1 4SP, +44 (0)114 203 9395, www.sheffield.gov.uk/libraries, archives@sheffield.gov.uk | Getting there A short walk from Sheffield Station, past The Cutting Edge sculpture up to Sheaf Street, then left | Hours Mon, Tue & Sat 9.30am–5.30pm | Tip Mugen Tea House, The Hide, Scotland Street, has a permanent display of photographs of Carpenter and various items produced in his praise.

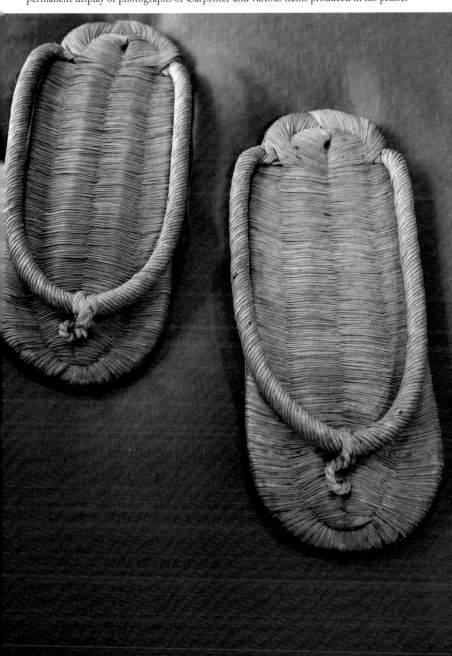

28 Emergency Services Museum

Inside the notorious murderer's dank cell

The National Emergency Services Museum, once a Victorian police-cum-fire station, lovingly wraps itself around the bottom corner of West Bar Green. Brilliant red vintage fire trucks nudge at its windows. Cast-iron ornamental brackets for hanging lamps depend purposelessly above the main façade. Just in front of the entrance, a full-size mannequin of a bored policeman sits in a chair behind a desk out of the 1920s, cigarette between his fingers. Inside, the history of the Yorkshire Constabulary begins with a display of old cabinets – everything is a bit fusty about this place – containing coppers' dusty grey notebooks and ledgers of photographs of sad criminals, each one holding up a blackboard with a written record of their crime. The pitiful woman you squint at through slightly besmirched glass reads: *Marion Batt, Larceny, 19.5.24.*

Just around the corner at your back, there's a dark corridor where the old police holding cells miserably lurk. Suddenly, everything begins to feel and smell cold, dank and slightly urinous. The first of these contains a mannequin of Sheffield's most notorious 19th-century murderer and cat burglar, Charlie Peace, a near-midget of a man with legs drawn up, huddled beneath an old grey blanket. Is the air a grimy yellow? It certainly feels that way. In a nearby cabinet, a letter confirms the authenticity of Peace's muzzle-loading percussion pistol, and, next to it, his spectacles, which look a bit fine and finicky, as if he might have posed as a man of discrimination. Well, he was a bit of a poser, from first to last. He played fancy violins from Cremona. He was also a dealer in antiques and, oh yes, a picture framer. His ladder for shinning up walls leans nearby. He also had lots of fine tools: jemmies, a small lantern for giving out precious little light.

Address Old Police / Fire Station, West Bar, S3 8PT, +44 (0)114 249 1999, www.emergencymuseum.org.uk, info@emergencyservicesmuseum.org.uk | Getting there 15-minute walk from bus and train stations; bus 81, 82, 85 or 86 from Arundel Gate; tram to Castle Square, then walk down Angel Street, Snig Hill and West Bar; or car: just off A 61, north of city centre, Workhouse Lane car park | Hours Wed–Sun 10am–4pm | Tip Just a 10-minute walk away, Paul Waplington's remarkable brick mosaic, *Steelworker* (1986), fills an entire gable end at the top of Castle Street.

29 _Ernest Wright and Sons

Putter-togetherers for five generations

At the back counter of this tiny, marvellously cluttered factory, which once played host to a glazier's business, Jamie and Faye are packing hand-crafted scissors into Jiffy bags as fast as human hands can move. Ernest Wright and Sons have been in the scissor-making business for five generations, but Nick Wright, the great-grandson of the firm's founder, oversaw the transformation of their fortunes in the summer of 2014 when a film by Shaun Bloodworth called *The Putter*, about the hand-crafting of scissors by one of their two vintage putter-togetherers (that's the trade name for a scissor-maker), went viral on the web. On Friday Nick had laid off two of his very few staff (there are just five of them making scissors here, and two are apprentices); by Monday everything had changed. Within a single week they had received enough orders to keep them busy for a year.

They make 120 different products, from the tiniest of nail scissors to 13-inch tailor's shears, and every part of the making process (apart from the raw-forged half scissors, which are bought in) happens either in this little workshop reeking of oil, overlooking the street or in the scruffy, windowless rooms behind the greasy orange curtain at the back. Only carbon (not stainless) steel is used because it holds its edge so well. First comes the tapping and the drilling, and next the flame-hardening of the blades in furnaces that are 50 years old. The scissors emerge dirty and rusty, so they need to be thrown into an alarmingly juddery machine called a rumbler, which is full of what look like tiny ceramic Tic Tacs, for rubbing and polishing. After they are thoroughly dried, the inside edges are ground, one at a time. After this, it's all manual work. The front shop is full of scissors sticks, glazing wheels, pillar drills. In all, five busy people make 15,000 pairs a year.

Their deft fingers move in a blur of making.

Address 58 Broad Lane, S1 4BT, +44 (0)114 204 1363, www.ernestwright.co.uk, enquiries@ernestwright.co.uk | Getting there Tram to City Hall, then walk down and turn right on Trippet Lane, right again onto Bailey Lane, final right onto Broad Lane | Hours Mon–Fri 9am–5pm | Tip Marvellously rough and ready, Fagan's is just across the road, excellent for its beer and its live music-making.

30_ Forge Bakehouse

Conjuring the Peaks from a storm of flour

'Sourdough, that's our house speciality,' Martha Brown announces, pausing breathlessly between one and another of her many jobs on this hectic early Saturday morning down at the bakery. The cafe's full to the gunnels. They're queueing out of the door for the bread. At Martha's back, a young, doughy-fingered baker is pouring a white storm of organic stoneground flour, courtesy of Yorkshire Organic Millers, out of a huge white bag, causing a bit of a dusty looking pother. Glancing back at the flour in full flight, Martha says she's a very practical kind of a person. 'We're very fond of the flour from Shipton Mill, Gloucestershire too,' she confides, even though it feels like a bit of a betrayal not to be using stuff from the home county all the time. Her auburn hair is pulled back off her face. She grins an infectious grin. Her father's a London bus driver, and her mother's an academic. She enrolled as a student at a school of artisan food near Worksop, on the Welbeck Estate. University didn't feel right for her. She wanted to be doing things with her hands – including the interior design of Forge Bakehouse. She made the benches and the tables. She did the tiling, designed the lighting. She made little maquettes out of straw so that she could imagine how it would all fit together. And it does, very well.

Opened in November 2012, the bakery is on a corner site, and the fairly narrow seating area for an all-day brunch is tucked away around the side, facing the street. Martha herself runs courses in bread-making, sourdough and French baking. There are pop-up pizza nights. When you walk in, piled shelves of fresh-baked loaves, brown, crusty, shapely, with a heavenly odoriferousness, face you side on, with marvellous names evocative of Sheffield and its countryside – Millstone, White Peak, Dark Peak... They seem to be leaning invitingly towards you, whispering: *choose me.*

Address 302 Abbeydale Road, S7 1FL, +44 (0)114 258 8987, www.forgebakehouse.co.uk, info@forgebakehouse.co.uk | Getting there Bus 76, 97 or 98 to Mother of God Catholic Church; or car: take A621, on-street parking nearby | Hours Mon–Fri 8am–4pm, Sat & Sun 9am–4pm | Tip If it's the evening hour, Picture House Social – in the basement of Abbeydale Picture House at 383 Abbeydale Road – is good for a cocktail, a pizza and a heady blast of live music.

31__ The Famous Sheffield Shop

The gleam and the glint of local metalware

Everywhere you look in this little shop, your eye catches the gleam and the glint of metalware, all Sheffield-produced and Sheffield-sourced. There are tankards, in pewter or silver, pruning knives, pocket knives, ferocious Bowie knives (gulp), saws, steels for making any carving knife's edge keen, all carefully hanging from hooks, or sitting neatly on shelves, or ranged in waist-high wooden display cabinets which tilt up towards you, fanning out beckoningly. The shop was started in 1983 by a local man called Don Alexander, who took redundancy from the steel industry at the age of 47 and decided to put that money into a business of which he knew he could be proud: selling the kind of hand-forged metalware for which Sheffield has been world-famous over centuries.

In 2001, Don retired and sold the shop to Paul Iseard, an honorary Sheffielder (even his well-cut grey suit has a slight metallic sheen to it) from elsewhere (Bournemouth), who has diversified the business somewhat. He lectures on the history of cutlery design, and even designs the stuff himself. He shows off two steak knives, inviting me to test the balance of each of them in my hand. One has a wooden handle, the other plastic. How does that feel to you? he enquires, scrutinising my response to his products with the wary eye of the expert. Sheffieldware from this shop travels to all points of the globe – there's a map of the world behind Paul's computer to which he directs my attention. It bristles with colourful, bobble-headed pins marking all the far-flung destinations of his stock, from Greenland to the South Pole. The shop also supplies steak knives to Claridge's and various Michelin-starred restaurants. They can't fill the Jiffy bags fast enough. The elderly lady who has just walked in needs her kitchen knife's edge restored. Manager Joanne deftly inserts it into the Catrasharp knife sharpener.

Address 475 Ecclesall Road, S11 8PP, +44 (0)114 268 5701, www.sheffield-made.com |
Getting there Bus 81, 82, 83, 83a or 88 from Leopold Street to Ecclesall Road near
Hickmott Road; or car: take A 625, on-street parking near Hunters Bar roundabout |
Hours Mon – Sat 9.30am – 5.30pm | Tip Thirsty for a local craft beer? Try The Beer House,
a micro-pub just doors away at 623 Ecclesall Road.

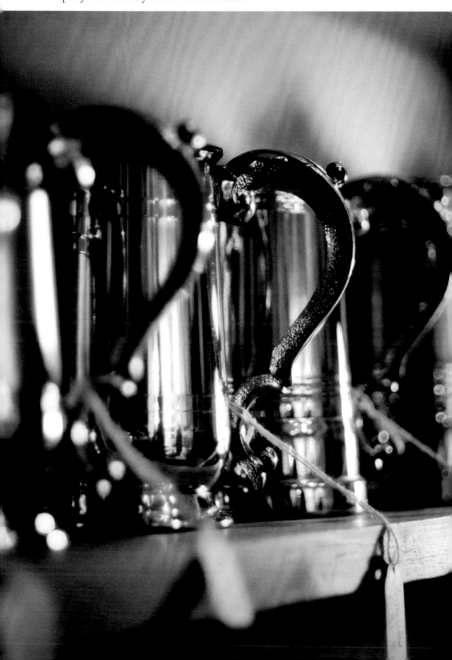

32 Frog Walk

The gennel overlooking the ancient snuff mill

What exactly is a gennel? Folks from Sheffield will tell you that it's their very special word for a walkway, often covered. It can lead you into a backyard common to a handful of terraced houses. At other times, it runs behind gardens, with perhaps a high stone wall on the other side. If you look over that wall, you might see a tree-shrouded embankment leading down to a modest stream. A gennel can be a meeting place for two people who fancy each other, or just a pleasurable way of getting somewhere. It usually feels quite private. Sometimes gennels overlook fascinating places – as does this one, which is called Frog Walk.

Frog Walk is a downhill walk or an uphill one, depending upon the direction you choose to take. It's not very long. It twists. It plunges, not too heart-stoppingly though. It has its surprises. If you start at the top, you will see, just before you take your first steps downhill, one of Sheffield's most remarkable surviving businesses, Wilson's old snuff mill, partly encircled by its own mill pond. Wilson started this business in the 1730s, and the same family makes snuff in the same little factory to this day. Inside there are the old workings that were used in the 18th century, ancient mortars and pestles encrusted with old snuff. It looks an idyllic scene from where you are watching – note the lovely, ancient sycamore on the higher bank of the pond. To the left, there is the Georgian house that was built to provide accommodation for the owners.

Now walk downhill. Soon the vista will open up on the left, and you will see Porter Brook hurrying downstream, that river which, when diverted into mill ponds, enabled small-scale industry to survive right up the valley. Moments later the brook will lead you to a remarkable stone portico, which you will now be seeing, side-on: the pompous entrance to Sheffield's General Cemetery.

Address Frog Walk, S11 8ZA, off Sharrow Vale Road | Getting there Bus 81, 82, 83, 83a or 88 from Leopold Street to Ecclesall Road near Hickmott Road, then walk down Hickmott Road to Sharrow Vale Road; or car: take the A 625 to Hunters Bar roundabout and turn onto Sharrow Vale Road, on-street parking | Hours Unrestricted | Tip Perfectionery at 255 Sharrow Vale Road sells mouth-watering cakes.

33_ The Full Monty
Hot Stuff kicking up a storm

Certain films seem to define the nature of a place. The reputation of Sheffield, for good or ill, pivots about a low-budget film set more than 30 years ago and filmed on location in the city. That film was The Full Monty, and it became a surprise global success. This film still divides local opinion. Some argue that its spiritedness, its pluck, its indomitable cheek in the face of the dying of Sheffield's great industries – coal and steel – did nothing but good. Nonsense, argue others. It was a bleak tale, with the flimsiest of gags for a storyline. Like it or not, The Full Monty is still an inescapable reference point – you could spend an entire day revisiting its locations, from the windy bleakness of Skye Edge, where the lads kicked a ball around, to the once horribly polluted Tinsley Canal.

Best of all is the local Labour Exchange on West Street, looking much as it did then from the outside. This is where the lads were said to have picked up a shoulder-nudging rhythm as they queued and listened to Donna Summer singing 'Hot Stuff '. The location remains a hot one to this day. There's no better place to wander in than West Street on a Saturday night. Flimsily clad kids shiver and caterwaul on cold winter days. Students come spilling downhill from Sheffield University, filling up the most bizarre of boozers. Take Walkabout, for example. Once the handsomest and most dig-nified of Sheffield's Methodist chapels, it is now like a building in crisis. The ground floor is all glitzy bar, fat chairs, and giant screens. Raise your eyes just a little, and you will see an entirely different world: a mahogany pulpit, from whose elegant vantage point some ghostly preacher thunders his disapproval. But was the scene really shot inside this job centre? No, it was a bit of deception on the part of the filmmaker. It was filmed at the Burton Street Foundation in Hillsborough.

Address Bailey Court, 112 West Street, S1 3SY | **Getting there** Bus 95 to West Street; tram to West Street; or car: Q Park Rockingham Street car park | **Hours** Unrestricted from outside | **Tip** Good food, music and excellent local beer? The Harley is five minutes' walk away at 334 Glossop Road.

34 The General Cemetery

Locals out of love with the catacombs

The General Cemetery's monumental, neoclassical gates take you aback: by their almost overbearing size, and everything that they seem to be saying about the importance of those who were buried here at a time, in the middle of the 19th century, when Sheffield was evolving into a great industrial city. It brings to mind the cemeteries of Paris or Rome. Inside these gates, a series of modest pathways lead you through a tiny landscape of great and ever-changing drama, with gentle declivities followed by steep, and suddenly ever steeper, hill climbs. This is an artfully man-crafted landscape – much of the stone used here was quarried from this site.

A meandering path beside the rushing Porter Brook takes you beside the catacombs, all bricked up, which rise up to the right in a great curving wall, parapetted, balustraded, at the top. These catacombs were not much loved by Sheffield folk. Few wanted them. They were expensive for a start – and who craves anonymity in death when he possesses the wherewithal to opt for pomp? Everywhere, amongst the ferns and the trees, there are monumental gravestones, some upright still, others leaning, yet others fallen flat on their faces or broken in half. Part of the appeal of this place is its heart-rendingly tragic near-ruinousness. The dead, pathetically, seem to be trying to outdo each other in the size and importance of their memorials. Look at the towering monument to the industrialist and philanthropist Mark Firth. The urn rises up from its plinth in a great, self-congratulatory flourish; and bounding that monument, railings cast in his own works. One of the less splendid, and all the more touching for that, is the gravestone marking the burial spot of Samuel Holberry, Sheffield's Chartist leader, who died in 1842 in York Castle at the age of 27 for fomenting insurrection in the service of political reform.

Address Cemetery Avenue, S11 8NT, +44 (0)114 268 3486, www.gencem.org, sgct@gencem.org | **Getting there** Bus 81, 82, 83, 84 or 88 from Leopold Street to Tesco on Ecclesall Road; or car: take A 625 (Ecclesall Road), and turn left into Cemetery Avenue, on-street parking | **Hours** Consult website for opening times and events | **Tip** Try the Ashoka Indian Restaurant at 307 Ecclesall Road for a good, wood-smoked tandoori.

35 The Golden Post Box

Honouring Jessica, history's greatest heptathlete

How should we honour our heroes? Gold is our most precious metal. Kings have often been anointed with crowns of gold. Poets and lovers have been known to write, or to mutter *sotto voce*: *you are more precious to me than gold*. Sporting heroines are given gold medals.

There have been many Sheffield sporting greats, from Sebastian Coe to Roger Taylor, from Gordon Banks, England's goalkeeper when the World Cup trophy was lifted in 1966, to Joe Root, current captain of the England cricket team. When Dame Jessica Ennis-Hill, Sheffield's star of track and field, and the most decorated heptathlete in history, won gold twice for Britain at the 2012 Olympics, the City of Sheffield decided to celebrate her achievements by painting a post box at the corner of Holly Street and Division Street gold. For a sportswoman who would have known the meaning of thirst when performing in the open air, it seems entirely fitting that this post box should be overlooked by a number of stone water-gods, all reliefs that help to embellish the façade of the handsome, mid-19th-century building which once housed the Sheffield Water Works, and which in style could be described as Sheffield's only answer to an Italian palazzo. The building still exists to quench the thirsts. It is now a Wetherspoon's pub.

Ennis-Hill, retired now from all that life-long intensive training, still lives and works in the city of her birth. She has exchanged the rigours of the track for the challenge of the pen and has written a series of seven books for children called *Evie's Magic Bracelet* with children's author Elen Caldecott. Otherwise, life is now less stressful and a little more pain-free than in those days of high-octane competitiveness. She swims with her son, Reggie. She does yoga regularly. She walks her dog in the woods near her home in Sheffield. She has melted back into the community with a sigh of relief.

Address At the Barker's Pool end of Division Street, S1 4GF | **Getting there** 15-minute walk from Sheffield Station or Interchange up Howard Street, along Surrey Street, and then, having crossed the road, up Barker's Pool, where the post box is situated at the far side of the City Hall | **Hours** Unrestricted | **Tip** Simmonites, Sheffield's best wet-fish counter, is directly across the road.

36__Granelli's

Sweets for the sucking since 1874

Granelli's old-fashioned sweet and spice shop has stood on this same site, at the bottom of a steep hill, and now close to one of Sheffield's busiest inner-city roundabouts, for 145 years, as one of Sheffield's most toothsome, transgressive delights. The neon-lit windows blaze with suckable promises, heaped up, pressing forward against the windowpanes, like an entire ravishing chorus line of *Eat Me! Eat Me!* The sweets themselves, shocking pinks, blues and greens in colour, and often over-layered with a snow-like veneer of sugar, are displayed in crinkly, sweet-bulgy polythene bags or tall, screw-top jars. Almost everything seems to cost 90 pence for 100 grammes. The names alone excite the sugar-eager palate: *Vanilla Fudge, Mini Mallows, Rainbow Crystals, Bargain Wine Gums, Fizzy Cola Bottles…*

Julian Granelli, son of Rosita, the current owner, tells me the story of how Genoese ice-cream maker Luigi Granelli came to Sheffield in 1874, understanding not a word of the language, all that local thee-ing and thou-ing. The Sheffield weather froze him stiff. His beard grew waist-length. He had a plan to teach Sheffielders to make ice cream, which Granelli's still make and sell to the original recipe. The sweets came later. Sweets were for winter. In those days they delivered by horse and cart. Little has changed inside the shop in the past half-century. It's a small, box-like, brightly lit space, with the sweets towering on shelves that climb as high as the ceiling. The space in front of the counter is so narrow that it's quite difficult for two people to push past each other. This squeezy boxed-inness seems to add to the excitement. Customers, usually with squirmily excitable, jab-by-fingered small children in tow, take an age to build up an order. Each small helping is poured into a little white paper bag, which gets a quick screwy twist at the top once full…

And perhaps a little more of the Yorkshire Mixture please…

Address 66–68 Broad Street, S2 5TG, +44 (0)114 272 2981 | Getting there Ten-minute walk from Sheffield Station. Turn right along Sheaf Street as far as Park Square Roundabout. Broad Street is the second road on the right. | Hours Mon, Thu, Fri 10am–4pm, Tue 10am–5.30pm, Sat & Sun 10am–5pm | Tip Just a few doors up the road, at 82 Broad Street, there's a very serious shop called Magick Enterprises.

37_ The Graves Gallery

Jane Austen's great-uncle in a candyfloss wig

The sober, avuncular likeness of Alderman W. G. Graves, one of Sheffield's greatest philanthropists, whose fortune was made in mail order, is displayed in the art gallery named after him above the Central Library in the city's best building of the 1930s (see ch. 14). Walk up to the third floor by the elegant staircase, with its lovingly polished brass handrail, which seems to turn and turn upon itself as it rises, ever upwards, in a kind of grave square dance.

The gallery itself shows off part of the city's fine art collections, which include works of great distinction, local, national and international, spanning the centuries, from Peter Lely to Jonathan Richardson, from J. M. W. Turner to Gérome, from Edward Burne-Jones to Stanley Spencer. The room devoted to portraiture is the best of all. Enjoy the marvellously blowsy likeness of Margaret Brooke by Peter Lely, court painter to Charles II. She may have died drinking hot chocolate laced with poison. Or, set neatly into an arched alcove, Jonathan Richardson's painting of that intrepid 18th-century traveller and writer Lady Mary Wortley Montague, thin-faced, neck stretched a little like a giraffe's. Admire also Ozias Humphrey's portrait of Jane Austen's great-uncle, the decidedly porcine Francis Austin Esq of Sevenoaks, with his silvery, candyfloss wig.

Or, nearby, Edward Burne-Jones' dreamlike *Hours*, in which the same model is used six times over to represent the peculiar, onward drift of time, ever similar, ever different. Also here is the haunting *A Corner of the Artist's Room in Paris* by Gwen John; it is all the more so for being so at odds with the common characterisation of this city as a place of smut, brass and nowt much else. Dated 1907–09, and of the utmost refinement, it shows a wicker chair beside a window in a quiet room. Through a haze of light, we look out over rooftops, our gaze ever expanding.

GALLERY II

Address Surrey Street, S1 1XZ, +44 (0)114 278 2600, www.sheffield.gov.uk/home/libraries-archives | **Getting there** Buses passing through city centre stop close by; tram to Castle Square; or by car: Q Park Charles Street car park | **Hours** Tue, Thu, Fri, Sat 11am–4pm, Wed 1–5pm | **Tip** At 70 Pinstone Street is a marvellous little bookshop, specialising in books from independent publishers and adventure magazines (www.labiblioteka.co).

38_Heeley City Farm
The child-friendliest of inner-city farms

What are children for? They exist to be brought to a place like this, a modest, small, slightly ramshackle inner-city farm on a hillside surprisingly close to the city centre, slotted neatly in between three rather steep and neglected side roads. Goats in a small, kerb-side field are the first animals to greet you, dropping you a few of their characteristic wild-eyed stares. Then, having crossed the road, you follow a fingerpost towards a low cluster of green wooden huts. Pathways are forever snaking here, there and elsewhere, as if they have only just made up their minds. Finding your way around and through this mazy place – everything is quite close-packed and richly interwoven – is itself a bit of a pleasing challenge to which you rise quite easily. Children, trailing random whoops, keep appearing and disappearing, flitty as dragonflies.

In one hut, Jerry the feral cat is sitting on a hay bale, minding his own business. A Sponsor's Board gives names of those who are helping with the upkeep. Sophie Tricklebank is supporting Summer the Pygmy Goat. Next up is a muddy-snouted, pink-eared pig, which is furiously rooting at huge pats of glistening black mud as if his life depended on it. Passing on to the rodents, you read the signage, so carefully expressed, such a model of casual, clear and perfectly calibrated child-friendliness, teaching children the first rudiments of up-quite-close animal husbandry: what to watch for, how to show care, how to approach without alarming. One chicken looks particularly sad. *This chicken is going through its summer moult,* you read. *She is also very old, so she may appear to look ill.* At road's edge, an exquisitely contented peahen sits with several companions in a large aviary, her plumage looking like a charcoal drawing of an exquisite piece of plumply rounded cloth, black strokes on white.

You'll be back, more kids in tow, in no time at all.

Address Richards Road, S2 3DT, +44 (0)114 258 0482, www.heeleyfarm.org.uk, info@heeleyfarm.co.uk | Getting there Bus 56 from Interchange to Prospect Road, Richards Road on left; or car: take A 61 (Chesterfield), turn left onto Myrtle Road, right onto Prospect Road, left onto Richards, on-street parking | Hours Daily 9.30am – 4pm | Tip Whirlow Hall Farm on Whirlow Lane can boast of an ancient cruck barn.

39 Helter-Skelter

A wild, helpless onrush, down and through…

There are two helter-skelters of significance in Sheffield. One is painted, and it hangs in the Graves Art Gallery (see ch. 37). Stanley Spencer's *Helter-Skelter* (1937), a painter's view from a window, is a shapely, melancholy thing, no longer a source of childlike wonderment. There are no people to be seen. It's boarded up, beyond useful life. Is it an image of the painter himself, in the grip of an inner crisis?

The helter-skelter that waits for you in the soaring atrium of the Electric Works just minutes from Sheffield Station is quite otherwise in its appeal. It's an invitation to participate in an adventure of displacement. The idea to install it here was Toby Hyam's, who runs a company called Creative Space Management. He'd seen Karsten Holler's slides at Tate Modern's Turbine Hall in London, and had recognised how what purported to be an art installation could morph into a thrilling, self-affirming, whole-body, slightly out-of-body experience, and decided that a city-centre office building whose focus would be upon attracting and encouraging new creative enterprises – from digital to media – could profit by such an attraction too.

You enter at third-floor level. The balcony enables you to take in the full extent of its dully gleaming, grey helix. It looks like a giant, fat, elegantly out-spooling worm as it descends through its 27.5 metres of length. Inserting your body into the metal entrance mouth is a little like entering a giant tubular caterpillar. Having slotted your feet into a sack which protects your shoes from slowing the descent, you lie yourself out flat (no raising of the head), stare at the ceiling, and let go. The seven-second descent is a great, helpless onrush, down and through, a no-holds-barred letting go through a plunging tunnel which, as you are about to touch bottom, makes a brutishly yanking, sideways swerve. Oh no! *Ah yes…*

Address Electric Works, Sheffield Digital Campus, S1 2BJ, +44 (0)114 286 6200,
www.electric-works.net, info@electric-works.net | Getting there 5-minute walk
from Sheffield Station, crossing road and turning right out of exit | Hours Mon–Fri
8.30am–5.30pm, by arrangement | Tip Just behind Electric Works, more physical
challenges lie in wait at the Ponds Forge International Sports Centre, which is open to all.

40__Henderson's Relish

The black stuff that defines the city

Certain people, products, places help to define a city. In the case of Sheffield, it is a relish called Henderson's, which first went on sale in 1885 (25 years later Henry Henderson sold the business on to a pickle manufacturer from Huddersfield). It added flavour to the kind of working man's meat and potato pie that was likely, in those days, to be more potato than meat. Hendo's – or 'the black stuff' – helped to give it kick, savour, spice, the taste its look and shape seemed to promise yet not quite deliver until the sauce was shaken on like a kind of magic dust. The city's devotion to its favourite relish was proven yet again recently when a Hendo's bottle was dug out of the ground on the battlefields of the Somme. What more comforting companion could there possibly be at a time of direst need?

The relish itself has been owned by the same family, the Freemans, since 1940, and that will continue into the future. Dr Freeman himself died in 2013 at the age of 93. His 84-year-old widow runs it now. The business operation is simple, efficient, and astonishingly small in scale. Six employees produce 660,000 bottles a year. Until recently, the bottling machine, bought second-hand in 1960, was in full operation. What is in the stuff though? The ingredients include cloves, cayenne pepper, vinegar, a special garlic mix, tamarind and water, and they are all mixed together, cold, in giant stainless steel vats. There is something else too: three secret ingredients, whose exact proportions are known only to three people. Each vat contains enough Hendo's to fill 3,000 bottles. What kind of weather do they prefer over at the factory in Darnall? Dreary, miserable weather, when the hot pies come out, and the arm effortlessly reaches across the table for the bottle of sauce that has become every Sheffielder's fast friend.

They even produce customised bottles. Saucy, eh?

Address Hendo's is almost everywhere, in restaurants, bars, and every branch of Wetherspoon's. It's even in the museum shops. | **Tip** Later on, you might want to sample a Bassett's liquorice allsort or two, also manufactured in Sheffield.

41 Jameson's Tea Rooms

An entire eighth of a cake to die for

The polka-dot bow-tied, straw-boatered waiters and waitresses flit about you like the meadow butterflies of high summer as you stare at the elegantly organised table settings, white tablecloths over blue on every table, suggesting that all is as ready as it could ever possibly be for a formal tea in the English tradition. The clock on the upright piano in the corner is topped by a bowler hat, cocked at a rather rakish angle. The music, not too loud, gently swings from textbook 1920s, created for wrist-twirling, fast-kicking flapper types, to the easy, velvety croon of Frank Sinatra. On the stroke of noon, the entertainment passes from recorded music to live when the pianist arrives. What are his favourites? Classics of the musical theatre, and sometimes brand new tunes, rendered in a surprisingly old-fashioned way. The maître d' stands by the entrance, leaning, with a slight air of languor, against a wooden lectern. There are pink roses on every table and baskets above the doorway. Two chandeliers hang overhead. The decor is an understated harmony of greys and whites.

The Jameson family, creators of this studiedly elegant tea room, started in business as dealers in antiques – that's why the tables and the chairs look so carefully chosen. Their speciality is afternoon teas – they offer 27 varieties of tea, including vanilla, wild cherry, mint and passion fruit – taken at an agreeably slow pace. Walk over to the counter and you can admire their selection of high-piled cakes on cake stands – 16 of them are on display today, bases cushioned by doilies. If you order a slice, you will not be knowingly under-provided-for. A slice at Jameson's means one-eighth of an entire cake. All the sandwiches and the scones are made on the premises. The local ham is hand-prepared. Clotted cream in plenty accompanies the jams. Heaven, in a nutshell.

Mark Jameson, cake-maker, is also a dab hand at French polishing.

Address 334 Abbeydale Road, S7 1FN, +44 (0)114 255 1159, www.jamesonstearooms.co.uk |
Getting there Bus 97 or 98 from Pinstone Street to Abbeydale Road South; or car: take
A 621, approximately 20 minutes from city centre | Hours Thu–Mon 10am–5pm | Tip
Swallows & Damsons, just a few doors away at 326 Abbeydale Road, is a florist selling
vintage flowers with the most nuanced colours.

42___Jarvis' Hard Night
Mouthing off in public places

There's a lot of public poetry about in Sheffield. Like a good bag of chips on a wet night, you can almost smell it. You spot it, for example, when you walk up steeply pitched Howard Street from Sheffield Station. The words on the side of that building, which belongs to Sheffield Hallam University, are by Andrew Motion, a recent poet laureate of these islands. Another poem, written by Simon Armitage, flings itself down a wall at Weston Bank. Being out in the air, it's about the air itself. It's also – at least in part – about how poems keep the language clean. Or, as the Irish poet Seamus Heaney once put it, how a good poem rinses the language.

One of the mouthiest bits of public verse out in the Sheffield air is on a wall in Boston Street, and it's by Sheffield's very own Jarvis Cocker, sometime lead singer of Pulp. This is the smelly-fingered lad who once worked on a fish stall in Sheffield Market, and tried to get rid of the cod-reek before that all-important party by washing his hands in bleach. In Boston Street, on the wall of a university lodging house, Jarvis is musing on the pleasures of getting trashed on cider. Fashioned from brushed steel, the words jump off the wall.

But public poetry in Sheffield goes back much further than that. At the bottom of Weston Park, there's a statue of the 19th-century local poet Ebenezer Elliott. Now even though Ebenezer didn't exactly live to see his poems displayed on the sides of public buildings, he did make poetry that was meant to be shouted out loud. His poems about the need to abolish the Corn Laws (a tax on bread) in order to prevent the poor becoming even poorer were furious public attacks on the politicians of the 1830s, and if Ebenezer was with us now, he'd want to see them up there in the air with all the rest of the loud, open-air talk and gostering you can hear in this blabbiest of cities.

Address Boston Street, S2 | Getting there Bus 75, 76, 97 or 98 from High Street and Pinstone Street to first stop on London Road, then walk along London Road and turn left at lights onto Boston Street; or car: take B 6388 (London Road) from ring road | Hours Unrestricted | Tip Harrison's Camera Shop, the best in Sheffield, is just up the street, at 112–114 London Road.

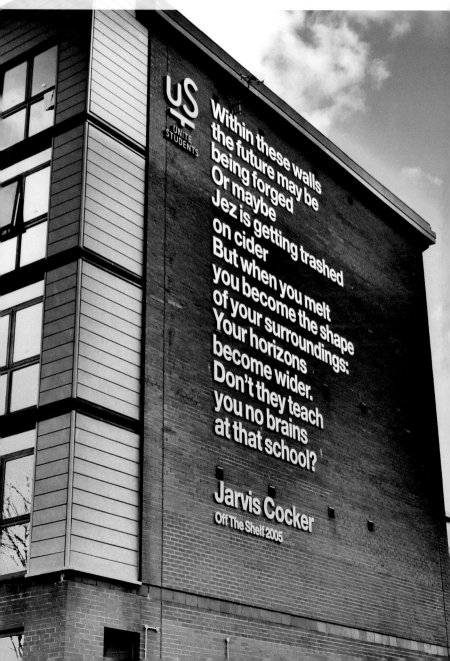

43_Jenkin Road
The steepest hill climb of the Tour de France

Why did the Tour de France of 2014 go through the old industrialised east end of Sheffield? One of the reasons might have been that its route included Jenkin Road, which sweeps up from the bottom of the Don Valley, and then climbs up the side of Wincobank Hill, that ancient site with its Roman Ridge and its Iron Age Hill Fort, so often misused in the past as a slag heap. This road, lined by suburban semis, was the steepest hill climb of the entire tour. An unlovely urban street with a relatively unprepossessing name became famous worldwide for the ferocious challenges that it posed.

It also serves to remind us that Sheffield, thanks to its unique topography – so suddenly inclined to uprear or side-swerve or downward-swoop – is one of the greatest and most ceaselessly inventive of cycling cities – in part, it has to be said, because of the extraordinary unpredictability of the landscape, mined and shaped by such river valleys. Take Jenkin Road itself, for example, and how it serpentines uphill, flattens out a little, and then suddenly uprears like a startled bolting horse, just as you think you understand its moods… There are bits of Sheffield perfectly suited to the most courageous of mountain bikers – the very top of Wharncliffe Crags, for example, to the north, where, plodding alone (or so you think), you suddenly catch flashes of red, yellow, blue Lycra through the mist, yards in front of you: lean, young, helmeted bikers, surging in close packs, quite slowly, weaving fat front wheels between treacherously slippery stones, which are often covered with the most brilliant green lichen. Or catch a few older Lycra'd ones ripping fast and arrow-straight along the Ringinglow Road. Later, legs spread, they sup pints of bitter in the Norfolk Arms.

Where to begin? As a visitor, pick up a bike for hire from the Cycle Hub outside Sheffield Station.

Address Jenkin Road, S9 | Getting there Bus X78 to Meadowhall, then a 9-minute walk to Jenkin Road; tram to Meadowhall terminus; or car: take A6109 out of the city, then turn left into Jenkin Road, on-street parking nearby | Hours Unrestricted | Tip Two-thirds of your sweaty toil uphill, Wincobank Common opens out to the right of you where you can enjoy a picnic and panoramic views.

44_ Kelham Island

Where old grit meets new shine

Kelham Island is not an island at all. It's a neighbourhood penned between the River Don and a goit – a local word for a mill race – which once teemed with small factories and workshops: cutlers, leather workers, steel manufacturers. The buildings these Victorian manufacturers created are amongst the most handsome survivals of Sheffield's industrial heritage. In recent years, many of them have been brought back into use for a variety of purposes, commercial and residential. A former power station beside the Don now houses the Kelham Island Museum, the country's best museum of industrial heritage. The 130-year-old Chimney House next door is as flexible as they come these days. You can fine-dine there – or marry.

The old has also made space for the new. Handsome new apartment blocks have deftly inserted themselves beside the Don. The pubs on Kelham Island are amongst the most Camra-decorated in Sheffield. Yellow Arch Studios (see ch. 5), where the Arctic Monkeys cut their milk teeth, has, over a decade and a half, been expanding into the buildings of a Victorian factory which once made giant nuts and bolts. An old steel works has been repurposed as a nerve-jangling indoor skatepark, with work by some of Sheffield's best-known street artists scattered about the walls to add to the pep and the mock-menace. The consequence of all this hectic entrepreneurial activity is that the island, which was semi-derelict and moribund half a century ago, is now a thriving community of livers and toilers and makers, young, middling and old. The island hosts markets regularly. And the Don, which once ran slow and sludgy with vivid-hued industrial pollutants, has come alive again. Tench swim in its waters. A heron can be seen from the waterside terrace of the Gardener's Rest up Neepsend way, topmost-branch-perching, waiting for its moment to strike lucky.

Address Kelham Island, S3 | Getting there Bus 7, 8 or 8a from Arundel Gate to Nursery Street (opposite Harlequin pub) then cross river and walk along the river path to Kelham; tram to Shalesmoor, then short walk down Green Lane and Alma Street | Hours Unrestricted | Tip Some of Sheffield's most handsome glazed tiles can be seen on the façade of the Ship Inn, 312 Shalesmoor. Good food and drink indoors too.

45__ The Kelham Island Tavern

Pleasingly adrift on a foaming head of cask ale

There are few sights more pleasing to the thirsty, when day edges down towards evening, than a battery of taps advertising a range of locally produced cask ales. Over at the Kelham Island Tavern, several-times winner of the Camra Award for best pub of the year, there are 13 cask beers on offer on any single night, most of them produced by the city's own breweries. Tonight's include Farmers Blonde, Barnsley Bitter and Deception.

The quality and sheer range of its cask beer culture is one of Sheffield's untold stories. There are 23 breweries in the city and many of them employ fewer than five people. Most of these local beers are made and sold within the region, so you need to come here to experience them.

The Kelham Island Tavern, with its wheel-back chairs, stoutly dependable wooden tables, a Tiffany light shade and invitingly warm, mustard-yellow walls, is a place that seems to welcome idling over a pint or two of beer with a good head. A shock-haired older man in a matelot's top is nursing a half. An eager mongrel is watching an entire table's lively conversation, switching its head from side to side. The beer mat on which you settle your pint is from the Double Top Brewery, beer makers since 2010, and it promises that the product *will hit the spot*. And it does. Another mat, courtesy of the Mallard, Worksop, advertises a local summer beer festival with up to 16 real ales and 3 real ciders. The prints on the walls – a demonic scene by Hieronymus Bosch; a dark blue night outside a cafe, complete with blazing stars, by Van Gogh; a Modigliani nude; botanical illustrations – are beer-friendly, reverie-inducing. There is a pretty outdoors seating area, over-hung with flowering shrubs. Empty aluminium casks of Abbeydale Brewery barrels wait beside the wall for collection. A pork pie and a pint of ale will cost less than a fiver.

Address 62 Russell Street, S3 8RW, +44 (0)114 272 2482, www.kelhamtavern.co.uk |
Getting there Bus 7, 8 or 8a from Arundel Gate to Nursery Street (opposite Harlequin
pub), then cross the river and walk along the river path to Kelham; tram to Shalesmoor, then
cross road and walk down Green Lane and Alma Street; on-street parking | Hours Fri &
Sat noon – midnight, Sun – Thu noon – 11pm | Tip If you want to turn this into a beer crawl,
the Fat Cat is waiting just across the street.

46__ The Lantern Theatre

A gift to a Soho-hungry daughter?

Some theatres spring up in the oddest of places. The smallest and oldest of Sheffield's theatres sits on a small triangle of land, pinched between two handsome Victorian houses, on a quiet, tree-lined street in Nether Edge. Is it a folly or not? The building resembles an off-kilter Swiss chalet, except that its roof is topped by a lantern. The walls are part decorated with terracotta tiles, slightly bitten at. What exactly is it doing here?

One plot line runs like this. The Lantern Theatre was built in 1893 on the land of the cutlery magnate whose house it now neighbours. It was a gift to his daughter, who wanted to be an actress. That would have meant going to London, and perhaps mingling with women of ill repute in dangerous theatreland. And so he built her a theatre of her own, and he called it the Chalet Theatre. The other plot line is that he had a passion for American vaudeville, and dreamt of savouring his own little slice of it just outside the door. By the 1950s the theatre was decrepit. Fortunately, a local drama teacher called Dilys Guite spotted it. It was owned at that time by Charles Ebenezer Richardson, who leased it to her for £1 a week. After the first performance – of Shakespeare's *Merry Wives of Windsor* – the owner gave the land to the Dilys Guite Players. The theatre was re-named after its odd lantern, and today it thrives with the help of a small army of voluntary labour. This is the only theatre troupe in Sheffield to own its own theatre.

The inside is a tiny scale model of a Victorian theatre (it seats just 84 people, 64 in the stalls and 19 in the balcony), complete with proscenium arch, and rich maroon walls. All the props are made here, in the workshop at the back. The Green Room is in the old stable block, which requires walking from one building to another. On rainy days, pick up an umbrella before you prepare to step on stage.

Address 18 Kenwood Park Road, S7 1NF, +44 (0)114 255 1776, www.lanterntheatre.org.uk, info@lanterntheatre.co.uk | Getting there Bus 3 from Arundel Gate (Hallam University) to Montgomery Road (bottom of Kenwood Park Road); or car: take A 625, then left onto Summerfield Street just past Waitrose | Hours Consult website for calendar of events | Tip If you are mad about community theatre, try the Merlin on Meadow Bank Road (www.merlintheatre.org).

47_Laundry

Hair-styling to the odour of warm towels

Hairdressing salons are curiously uniform places, all fake gloss and shininess, and usually squeezed into spaces too small for comfort. When Mitchell Wilson came to Sheffield 20 years ago – though born on a red-brick housing estate in Leicester, he'd been a stylist for Toni and Guy in London – his first thought was this: think of a name which has no connection with hair, and which might be evocative of the warm, nurturing smell of towels being spun in a laundry…

The rest of the dream was made up from scratch and recycled industrial scraps, with Mitch the all-jobs-man working on site with Reg the retired welder from Hillsborough.

You enter by a slender cafe, where the floor with its intriguing flecks of colour is from a school gym. Here you can take a freshly cold-pressed juice seated in a plump, yellow, recycled bus seat. That pink logo high on the wall is a running hare, and around it hares are chasing other hares. Hare or hair?

The space where the cutting is done is warehousily big, with warm, broad floorboards – 150 years old, from a 19th-century mill. The hanging lamps are industrial, newly powder-coated, the walls a rough-mortared red brick. A loveable-looking dog called Gizmo, a shih-tzu who belongs to Billy the stylist, is lying flat out on the floor in zig-zaggy formation, ready to be tripped over. Long central tables with polished concrete tops, steel-framed, all welded by Reg on site, run down the room. The mirrors are steel-framed too. It's all Hillsborough Steel stock, Mitchell tells me. Just off to one side there's a table rescued from the science lab at Bradfield School, and a butler's sink. Is that a slight smell of towels being laundered I detect on the air? Yes, the ducts from the laundry at the back do pump it through. That slight whiff of freshly laundered towels is indeed rather comforting…

Address 151 Sellers Wheel, Arundel Street, S1 2NU, +44 (0)276 3645, www.wearelaundry.co.uk, hello@wearelaundry.co.uk | Getting there 5-minute walk from Sheffield Station, past The Cutting Edge sculpture, up Howard Street, then left into Arundel Street | Hours Tue 9.30am – 6.30pm, Wed – Fri 9.30am – 7.30pm, Sat 9am – 5pm | Tip The free-to-enter exhibitions at Site Gallery, five minutes by foot from here at 1 Brown Street, are always inventive and thought-provoking.

48_ The Leadmill

Musical excess on the beery dance floor

Did the Aztecs ever play loud music? The sculpture above the street door of the Leadmill, in which a wild-jiving, note-spewing horn-blower seems to be challenging a spike-haired bassist to raise the roof just a little higher, might suggest as much. Indoors, the smell pricks at your nostrils as you climb the dour stone steps up to the offices above the main music venue: the pleasing reek of stale beer. This building, like so many in Sheffield, was built for one purpose and is now being used for another. In the 18th century, it made pigments for paint and pottery, but for the last 25 years it has been Sheffield's most celebrated live music venue, where such local bands as Pulp and Cabaret Voltaire have come of age. And it continues to diversify: into comedy, film screenings, club nights, theatre.

Once through the street door, you pass along a black corridor busily graffitied by Kid Acne, that celebrated Sheffield street artist. Down the walls you read off frenzied shower-bursts of words, tags, drawings evoking the names of everyone who has ever played here: *Don't Leave Me Hanging on the Telephone…On the Dance Floor…It's a Long Way to the Top if you Wanna Rock N Roll…*

Then, immediately, you are onto the dance floor itself, a wide semi-circle that can hold 900 heaving bodies (there's a smaller one at the back for the up-and-coming, which holds 250). Above your head, lights, lights, lights, swivelled in all directions, swing from a low-hanging gantry of silvery technical clutter. The brick walls are painted black. The gleaming wooden floor is newly washed of its slippery beery stickiness. A cash machine on the far wall invites impulsive excess. This is where, in July 2005, those local lads the Arctic Monkeys, who were just on the brink of global success, played, as they put it then, their 'best gig so far'.

Not so long before they'd been school kids from High Green.

Address 6 Leadmill Road, S1 4SE, +44 (0)114 272 7040, www.leadmill.co.uk, information@leadmill.co.uk | Getting there An easy walk from Sheffield Station: turn left along Sheaf Street (which becomes Shoreham Street), then left again onto Leadmill Road | Hours Mon–Thu 10am–5pm, Fri 10am–5pm & 11pm–4am, Sat 11pm–4am | Tip Try The Greystones on Greystones Road for yet more live music.

49___Legends of the Lane Museum

Troops watch the Blades thrash Chelsea

A football museum can be a place of marvels to dribble through. One of only a handful of its kind, Legends of the Lane opened as part of a new development at Sheffield United's ground in 2015.

Inside a large glass cabinet are displayed the photographs, cup winners' medals, match ball, official programme and much else which tell the story of a football match unlike any other. All this memorabilia records the Khaki Final, staged at Old Trafford on 24 April 1915, the only FA Cup Final ever to be played during a world war. In spite of the fact that Sheffield United defeated Chelsea by three goals to nil, there were no post-match celebrations in the city immediately afterwards, and precious little that was celebratory during the match itself. Almost all the crowd were soldiers, so the stands were filled with a sea of khaki. Cheering was discouraged. The weather was sullen. When the players arrived back at Sheffield Station with the cup under cover of the darkness of midnight – as the police had insisted – the players were all quietly ushered away in waiting taxis.

The objects in the cabinet remind us just how different football was back then. The match ball – a silver medallion is attached to it, naming the occasion and the surnames of all the members of the cup-winning team – is an ancient, battered, saggy, wrinkled patchwork of dark sewn leather, heavy enough to cause mild concussion when headed in miserably wet weather. The programme is extraordinarily wordy, with double columns of small print on every page. At least one member of the team – earnest, fresh-faced, more scholar than footballer – has his hair parted down the middle. The photograph of the winning team shows them all staring ahead, unsmiling, as a token of respect.

Address Bramall Lane, S2 4SU, +44 (0)114 253 7200, www.sufc.co.uk | **Getting there**
Bus 252 to Sheffield United Football Ground, 3, 43, 44 (Chesterfield) or 18 from Arundel
Gate; tram to Granville Road/The Sheffield College; or car: take Suffolk Street from Sheaf
Street roundabout, then at Granville Square roundabout, turn right onto St Mary's Road
and second left onto Shoreham Street and the ground is on right | **Hours** Open on home
matchdays only; consult website | **Tip** Wavelength Music at 165 London Road is Sheffield's
best guitar shop.

50__ The Leopold Hotel
Joe Cocker once sang his heart out

This Edwardian hotel at the city's heart has had several lives. Between 1907 and 1932 it was called Firth College, after the name of its founder, Mark Firth. Then, for over 30 years, it became a school, nicknamed Central Tech. Since 2006, it has been a boutique hotel of 76 rooms. Surprisingly, the school has hung on in the hotel. There are photographs of classrooms and groups of boys milling in corridors, the school's original staircase, and even a door sign which reads: *Headmaster's Study.*

Every few weeks, the old boys of Central Tech gather to exchange tales of past classmates, who have included the legendary England goalkeeper Gordon Banks, night-club impresario Peter Stringfellow, and, in a grainy shot halfway up a staircase which shows him with an unruly mop of tousled curls, Joe Cocker, England's greatest soul singer and air guitarist, looking small and slightly mischievous. About 14 years old, he doesn't look as if he's fitting in very well.

The headmaster of the time, Herbert Wadge, fierce, disciplinarian, doesn't seem like Joe's type either. 'Ex-Coldstream Guards,' Stuart, the secretary of the old boys' association, comments. 'He was a bugger, a real sod. But a good un.' What was Joe like as a schoolboy? Short and squat, one old boy remembers, 'dead opposite of his brother Vic, who was tall and academic.' What did Joe like doing as a schoolboy? Singing. All the time. His friends told him to shut up, but did he? What sort of songs? Blues numbers. The trouble was music wasn't an official subject, and Joe got himself into trouble for singing in the wrong place at the wrong time. He lived in a small terraced house in Crookes, and his parents were very ordinary people. Joe himself became a gas fitter after Tech. One old boy looks at another. 'Didn't he once come and replace the burners on your mother's cooker?' 'I believe that he did.'

Address 2 Leopold Street, Leopold Square, S1 2GZ, +44 (0)114 252 4000, www.leopoldhotel.co.uk, res.sheffield@leopoldhotels.com | Getting there The hotel is in the city centre, 10 minutes' walk from Sheffield Interchange or Sheffield Station; or tram from Sheffield Station to cathedral | Tip There's a bench in Leopold Square on which the names of famous Central Tech old boys are inscribed.

51 Manor Lodge

Where Mary, Queen of Scots sewed and schemed

Ancient abuts modern so suddenly. The Tudor Ruins, a medley of tumbling brick and grey stone, come into view directly beside the road – a towering chimney stack, walls bitten into like a crumbly cheese – as you reach the crest of the hill that dramatically overlooks the centre of Sheffield. Weaving your way into the site through the discretely positioned Discovery Centre, a coin-in-the-slot, wooden tableau of puppet-like characters cuts to the heart of the matter. Push in a 50-pence piece, and you will have the pleasure of seeing a kneeling queen losing her head to the executioner all over again.

This is one of the places in Sheffield where that potentially explosive Catholic, Mary, Queen of Scots, was incarcerated for 14 years. The 6th Earl of Shrewsbury, who owned this great manor house, had the dubious privilege of watching over her at huge expense to himself. Within three years of her leaving Sheffield, the plot she had hatched to overthrow Elizabeth I was uncovered, and off went her head.

The story of this house, the years of its prosperity, and its decline and fall into the ruins we see today, is told with restraint and family-welcoming skill as we walk through the site, peeling back the layers of history as we go. It is a little like meandering through a beautiful, untidy field. Meadow flowers in abundance have been planted beside the serendipitous path to the Turret House, the most complete survival of all. Before we reach that lodge's door, we will have walked beside a single wall of the Long Gallery, and then, having stood in the centre of the remains of Cardinal Wolsey's tower – he too was travelling south in the general direction of his death when he stayed here – we peer into Sheffield's oldest surviving lavatory, a two-seater, now lacking its wooden seat, which would have been rendered a touch more fragrant by sprigs of rosemary.

At your back, mixing then and now, a kiddie cartwheels wildly.

Address 197 Manor Lane, S2 1UJ, +44 (0)114 276 2828, www.sheffieldmanorlodge.org, visit@greenstate.org | Getting there Bus 56 from Pond Street (opposite Sheffield Interchange) to Boundary Road, then walk along Southend Road and turn left onto Manor Lane, or bus 120 from Sheffield Interchange to City Road and walk up Manor Lane; or car: take A6135 (Mosborough) from city centre, then from City Road turn left onto Manor Lane, on-site parking | Hours Visit website for limited opening times | Tip The wonderful homeyness of the Rhubard Shed Cafe is a short drive (followed by a left turn) down the road from here at 389 Manor Lane.

52__Marmadukes
Good food spiced with Sheffield wit

Norfolk Row is one of those small, traffic-banished, city-centre side streets – you can see Tudor Square and the city's main theatres from the middle of it – which feel like a haven of calm and sanity in a brawling world. The buildings on its south side are modest, two-storey, red-brick affairs, built in the 18th century for the most part, and 40 years ago this was solicitor-land, all shiny brass plates and closed doors. Now the smell of good food quickens the footfall. The north side of the street is the home of St Marie's, the handsome, 19th-century Roman Catholic cathedral, recently refurbished, in whose design the great architect Pugin had a hand – he even designed a chalice for the church.

On a fine day you can take breakfast or lunch on the pavement outside Marmadukes cafe, which faces the cathedral's bright-shining new railings. Marmadukes is the brainchild of a retired policeman and his wife, and it serves one of the best eggs Benedict with ham and toasted muffin on a no-nonsense enamel plate that a human being could ever hope to eat at 9am on a weekday morning. Or try scrambled egg on toast, lightly sprinkled with chives. The waiting staff come armed with keen-bladed Sheffield wit. Will there be cutlery to go with the food? 'You're not going to stick your face in it then?' the waitress replies. The entire place more subtly inveigles Sheffield in other ways, too. The floor tiles are colourful Moroccan (sourced in Bristol), but the sides of the counter beside the till are sheets of steel, as is the shelving. The benches at the tables are pinioned to the floor by steel bolts. The dining spaces inside are snug, intimate and a touch pleasingly unpredictable in their shapes. Marmaduke himself is a cycling bear, and he appears, smokily outlined in black, on the stripped-pine-panelled walls, scarf streaming, as he insouciantly pedals along.

Address 22 Norfolk Row, S1 2PA, +44 (0)114 276 7462, www.marmadukes.co | **Getting there** 1-minute walk from Sheffield City Hall, first right off the top end of Fargate | **Hours** Mon–Sat 8.30am–4pm, Sun 9.30am–4pm | **Tip** Look out for a poem by Roger McGough near the entrance to the Winter Garden just a couple of minutes' walk away off Tudor Square. The cheeky scouser twins Sheffield with Mars.

53 Museum of Gardening Tools

Meersbrook Park's Walled Garden Mess Room

Delilah the tabby flees on ahead of us, skittishly, and then plumps herself down near the entrance to the overarching willow tunnel at the centre of the old Walled Garden in Meersbrook Park. Kaktus, the garden's chief custodian of the day, mumbles that no one quite realised how often a willow tunnel would need to be trimmed: three times a year, he sighs, then laughs. The joke's on him. He also mentions something even more interesting. These old, red-brick, garden boundary walls – he points – have a snaking flue, which means that the walls were once heated by a coal fire to protect the plants against frost. This dates the garden to between 1810 and 1820. He points to the small green gate by which the butler from Meersbrook Hall would have entered for a quiet confab with the Head Gardener. Then, rapidly moving ahead with a bit of a lurching walk, he shows us other wonderful things: the Japanese garden, with its ginkgo tree; the herb garden; the precious metasequoia, planted in 1974, which started out as a seedling at Kew Gardens, and now flourishes here, on a rising bank.

Once this sequestered nook, at a levellish point on a hillside, was looked after by the council. People were trained here. Now its one-and-a-half acres of plots, trees, plants, flowers, shrubs and slightly decrepit greenhouses are loved and tended by a posse of tireless volunteers. The best things of all are in the old Mess Room, a mini-museum of gardening tools, some perhaps 200 years old. They sit on the floor, sometimes in buckets, or are displayed in elegant, fan-like shapes on the walls: a scythe once used for the terrible job of cutting wheat. (They had to work in strict lines to avoid cutting the Achilles tendon of the toiler in front.) There are jigging tools, cutting tools, hedge tools. And many, many old lawn mowers.

Address Chesterfield Road, S8, +44 (0)114 281 0423, www.meersbrookpark.co.uk |
Getting there Bus 43, 44 or X17 from city centre to Beeton Road, then walk up Beeton
Road right onto Brook Road, and 200 metres to park entrance; or car: take A61 (Heeley),
turn left at Beeton Road, right onto Brook Road | Hours Consult website for events and
opening times | Tip Bishops' House, a charming, timber-framed museum of c. 1500 is at the
southern end of the park.

54 Music in the Round

Flung headlong into music-making

Sheffield hosts several excellent music festivals, but only one of them, Music in the Round, is not limited to a particular season. What is more, the festival itself represents a unique experience in music-making and music-listening, thanks, in part at least, to its most regular location, the Studio Theatre at the Crucible. The Crucible, which opened its doors in 1971, was itself a bold and radical step in theatre-making. Its elongated stage, which thrusts deep into the auditorium, means that the audience is forever in the thick of the action, experiencing all the emotional maelstrom of headlong make-believe.

Something similarly intimate and informal happens in the Crucible Studio Theatre when Music in the Round is taking place. As the name of the festival suggests, the audience completely surrounds the players, in a tight circle. Much tighter than any Catalan bull ring – and quite as intense, though much less bloody. It is a festival of chamber music essentially – very few players are on stage at any one time. A singer, with piano accompanist, for example. A solo pianist. Or a string quartet. Its name and success as an experiment in the intimate presentation of intimate music – because chamber music is nothing but intimate – is synonymous with Sheffield's Lindsay String Quartet, which nurtured and participated in the festival over a period of almost 40 years. The Lindsays were themselves pure drama – they brought a thrill, an informality, and a dramatic emotional immediacy to whatever they were playing. The tight encirclement sets you, as an audience, uniquely at one with the music and the musicians. It flings you amongst them. The festival feels community-driven in spirit. This is no place for dickie bows or penguin suits. You wear a jumper. You roll up your sleeves. And the Lindsays' legacy is felt on the pulses to this day.

Address Howard Street, S1 1WB +44 (0)114 281 4660, www.musicintheround.co.uk, info@musicintheround.co.uk | **Getting there** Bus to Sheffield Interchange; tram to Castle Square; or car: Q Park Charles Street car park | **Hours** Consult website for show times | **Tip** Go and look up at the lovely low relief sculptures of working men on the façade of the White Building in Fitzalan Square five minutes' walk from here.

55__The National Fairground Archive

The day Buffalo Bill thundered through Sheffield

When, in 2001, the artist Jeremy Deller staged a re-enactment of the savage clashes that had taken place almost 20 years before between South Yorkshire Police and striking coal miners in the 'Battle of Orgreave', a pit village near Sheffield, critics praised it for being a startlingly innovative piece of art in motion. They had evidently forgotten that, almost 100 years earlier, an even more dramatic feat of historical re-construction had been staged in Sheffield itself, on a site just off the Penistone Road, close to where Sheffield Wednesday's football ground now stands.

Here, in 1891, Buffalo Bill, dime novelist, playwright, Indian scalper and consummate showman, with a company of 200 palefaces and a substantial posse of 90 genuine Sioux Indians, had reconstructed, in an arena constructed at great speed, such scenes from the great surge west as the following: a prairie emigrant crossing the plains, attacked by marauding Indians (who are, of course, repulsed); the Battle of San Juan Hill; Indians from the Sioux, Arrapahoe, Brule and Cheyenne tribes re-staging skirmishes or tribal dances. But before any of that could happen, 'The Star Spangled Banner' was played, solemnly.

The official, 64-page, 6-pence programme of Buffalo Bill's Wild West Show, which thundered through Sheffield for an entire week, can be examined at a remarkable, publicly accessible research resource held at the University of Sheffield called the National Fairground Archive. In addition to much information about Buffalo Bill and his inglorious history as a tamer and humiliator of Native Americans, the programme contains ads for Dunn's famous bowler hats (purchasable from 76 Sheffield High Street, and Wright's Coal Tar Soap, which, near miraculously, promised relief from smallpox and measles.

Address National Fairground and Circus Archive, University of Sheffield, Western Bank, S3 7NA, www.sheffield.ac.uk.nfca, info@sheffield.ac.uk | **Getting there** Bus 51, 52 or 52a from High Street to Western Bank; tram to University of Sheffield; or car: take A 57 (Glossop) from city centre, Q Park Durham Road car park | **Hours** Visit website for limited hours | **Tip** The old, red brick buildings of Sheffield University are a short walk uphill away. Go into Firth Court, and re-imagine the Oxbridge collegiate dreams of those who created it.

56_Now Then
The no-nonsense of street art

Street art is a here today, gone tomorrow sort of affair. And Shef-field is a city where it thrives. There are the internationally famous names who may have been here for years, all with suitably extrav-agant, undercover identities – Phlegm, Rocket, Kid Acne, Fauna-graphic, for example – and then there are the many younger artists fresh out of college.

Everywhere in this city you can see small, empty or semi-derelict factories where cutlers or silversmiths might once have worked, or hoardings surrounding a new building site. These are the places where the street artists tend to flock, often moving around in gangs. They save up for their cans of spray paint, they contact each other by social media, and then, sometimes with girlfriends in tow, they descend on a new target, often working at night, illicitly if it is a public building, with the girls posted on street corners, looking out for figures in authority. They are territorial. They backbite. They often work very fast indeed.

The kind of street art that you can see around Mary Street, Matilda Street and Arundel Gate, for example, can be highly sophisticated stuff. These artists are not taggers; they have grander ambitions. This lovely, colourful gable-end mural, called *Now Then*, is close to the top corner of Howard Street, and it presents us with a couple of words that are often on the lips of Sheffielders. (*Now Then* is also the name of a local magazine of independent-spirited commentary). It's a phrase with which to begin a conversation. Pay attention, pal, don't take us Sheffielders for granted…

How do street artists survive? Occasionally they get sponsorship from the university. Rupert Wood runs APG Gallery in Sidney Street and makes screen prints in multiples for sale through his gallery. Some Sheffield street artists don't like that. It smacks of selling out. These types are called 'art fags' by the real outlaws.

Address Corner of Howard Street, Sheffield | **Getting there** 5-minute walk from Sheffield Station, past the *Cutting Edge* sculpture, then straight up Howard Street | **Hours** Unrestricted | **Tip** Enjoy a free exhibition at the Millennium Gallery, two minutes from here.

57 — The Old Queen's Head

Sheffield's most venerable, saggy hostelry

The Old Queen's Head, Sheffield's most ancient hostelry, sits pinched into a corner – an unlovely location – next to the bus station on Pond Street. Made of lath, brick and timber at some time in the 15th century, it looks wheezy, saggy, as if it might be slowly settling into the ground. Its roof bows a little in the middle. It had a different name once: the Hawl at the Ponds, which means that there was a fishing pond nearby. Mary, Queen of Scots, who spent 15 years as a prisoner in Sheffield before her execution, may have dipped her toe into that pond. This site has been a transport interchange for centuries: inside the pub, you can see an old photograph advertising services by coach and horse to such far-flung places as Hathersage or London. It was built as a hunting lodge for Sheffield Castle, a structure that lasted until the end of the English Civil War. The castle was demolished as a way of punishing its commander for supporting the Royalists, but this building survived.

Some of its most interesting features are the large, rather ghostly heads, carved out of wood, which serve as corbels on the outside of the building. There are two more of them behind the bar. The two outdoors flank the long window of the principal façade. Is the female one a queen? She is crowned, and protected by a lovely canopy. Her partner to the right has his arms raised, as if doing his damnedest to keep the building up. With surprisingly prominent teeth, he is alarmingly bulbous-eyed – not quite so bulbous as the eyes of the head on the right-hand end of the bar indoors though, which looks as if it might have larger relatives on Easter Island in the Pacific. The ceilings loom low, the beams threateningly huge. Above a 16th-century fireplace, glass cabinets show objects scavenged during excavations: clay pipes, for example, pale as any shivery child's skin.

Address 40 Pond Hill, S1 2BG, +44 (0)7983 559073, www.theoldqueenshead.co.uk, info@theoldqueenshead.co.uk | **Getting there** 5-minute walk from Sheffield Station, through Sheffield Interchange and out to the end of Pond Hill | **Hours** Mon–Thu noon–10.30pm, Fri & Sat noon–11pm | **Tip** Just across the road from the Old Queen's Head survives the handsome arched stone entrance to Old Ponds Forge.

58 Our Cow Molly
Richest of ice creams from a herd of Friesians

High on a hillside overlooking Sheffield's Loxley Valley, in the ancient and earthily named township of Dungworth, sit a few fields of rich pasture land that have not seen a plough for at least 40 years. It was here, in 1947, that a farmer called Hector Andrew started his small dairy farm, and from where, for years, he used to trundle the crates of milk from his 10 cows, by horse and cart, into Sheffield and its surrounding villages. Three generations on, that same family is still keeping cows on this land, but the need to diversify in the face of an ever starker economic outlook caused them, in 2007, to start making ice cream with the best possible equipment and flavourings from Italy, and the best possible milk source – their own herd of mostly Friesians, which has now swollen to 90 (though a frisky red amongst them always insists on leading the herd into the field of a morning).

They renamed the enterprise Our Cow Molly, and the logo, in pink, white and black, which looks as if it might have been written in swirly liquid bubble gum, sums up the spirit of the endeavour: it is personable, comic and infectiously family-friendly. On a warm summer's day, the crowds come queuing here for a product which is as good as any gelato the world over. The cars line up in the field directly above where the cows are ranging. Having passed over a tight, steep wooden stile in a drystone wall, you can sit outside in the farmyard, at a pink-painted wooden table, enjoying a cone or two overloaded with Cora's Chaos (named after a daughter) or bubblegum or rhubarb and custard. What exactly is it about Our Cow Molly ice cream which makes it taste so good, though? Well, it does not give itself up to the pushing tongue too readily. It is so rich and so creamy that it requires a good deal of determined digging and delving.

Even the largest pots don't linger in the freezer.

Address Cliffe House Farm, Hill Top Road, Dungworth, S6 6GW, +44 (0)114 233 3697, www.ourcowmolly.co.uk | **Getting there** Bus 61 or 62 from city centre (Arundel Gate, Lyceum Theatre) and Hillsborough Interchange directly to Our Cow Molly; or car: take A 61, B 6076, then follow signs, parking in field | **Hours** Wed, Fri–Sun 11am–5pm | **Tip** Take a short drive into Lower Bradfield for a pleasurable stroll around the Damflask Reservoir.

59__Owlerton Stadium

Hurtling greyhounds and daredevil riders

We're almost off! The last odds have been chalked up on the three bookies' boards beside the track, and just before the next race begins – one happens every 15 minutes – a fashion parade of thin-legged, long-muzzled, mild-mannered greyhounds steps out, dressed in the coats that keep their well-toned muscles warm. Round and round they pace, in a wide circle, stepping finically, sniffing the evening air, led on by trainers hunkered down into their orange jackets.

A bell rings and, seconds later, a man steps out in front of the traps, and does a quick double flourish with a pair of flags. 'Ladies and gentlemen, the hare is on the move!' comes the silky voice over the tannoy. The mechanical hare, a small orange bullet, speeds smoothly past on the outside lane, and the dogs bolt out of their traps, lean, long-legged, forward-hurtling, going after that orange blur which never stops outpacing them around the oval perimeter. The flood lighting, harsh and flat, picks out the ads on the hoardings opposite, which seem to stand to attention as the dogs streak by: *Bet Fred*; *Napoleon's Casino*; *Bapp for Bolts.* And, a touch more melancholically: *Accept a Retired Greyhound.*

Inside, in the Hare and Hounds Bar, pints of bitter are being pulled, and loud-voiced men, big legs braced wide, stand their ground, in huddles. Others – the older ones – are sitting around tables with tiny blue pens, staring down at the day's Racing Guide, putting crosses against future favourites with their colourful names: Foxy Sally? Kowloon Peteball? Yahoo Benny? Everyone is the winner of someone's dream. At the Tote Window they are queuing up to bet: as little as £2 can bag you a winner.

It's been going on like this down at Sheffield's Owlerton Stadium since 1929, with dog racing in the winter months and speedway – those daredevils on brakeless bikes - in spring and summer.

Address Penistone Road, S6 2DE, +44 (0)114 234 3074, www.owlertonstadium.co.uk, enquiries@owlertonstadium.co.uk | Getting there Bus 7, 8, 8a or 86 from Arundel Gate to Penistone Road; or car: take A61 (Barnsley) from city centre and follow signs for stadium | Hours See website for hours | Tip The old Sheffield Barracks, where, in the Garrison Hotel, you can dine in a former prison cell, is five minutes' walk from here.

60 _ Paradise Square

Where the agitators once gathered

This is not a city of unbridled civic grandeur. There was no dramatic, 18th-century re-build here. Sheffield's only Georgian square is tucked in below the cathedral, and you can approach it down a steep, narrow, stone-paved lane called St James Row. The ground, as so often in this city, falls away suddenly as you walk downhill, and when you are perhaps 100 metres away, your eye-line is already on a level with the rooftops of the square and, beyond that, a wooded hillside. Even when embedded within the unrelentingly urban, there is a promise of nature here if you trouble to raise your eyes to the horizon.

The square itself, laid with chunky cobbles, and with a gas lamp standard at its centre, is relatively modest in size, and it seems, as it falls away downhill, to be lurching to the left a little like a drunk. The rooflines descend in jolting steps. Though a square, it does not exactly feel or even look quite like a square because it is built on such a steep hillside, which, unsurprisingly, was a cornfield before two builders called Nicholas and Thomas Broadbent created what, more or less, you see now. Those who occupy it are a quiet, mentally scheming, sober-suited mob these days – solicitors, tax consultants, chartered accountants – and the square itself feels quiet and serene.

Not so in the past. This square has known Chartist meetings peopled by hundreds of agitators. The plaques on the red-brick façades tell us some of its story: in one property lived David Daniel Davis, who assisted at the birth of Queen Victoria; in another, Sheffield's most celebrated sculptor, Francis Chantrey, had a studio, where as a young man he eked out a meagre living as a portrait painter. A house at the top of the square records the presence of John Wesley, who is said to have preached to the largest crowd he had ever seen in daylight hours.

The founder of Methodism was a consummate showman.

Address Paradise Square, S1 2DE | Getting there Follow St James Lane down the left side of the cathedral | Hours Unrestricted | Tip Sheffield's only triangular pub, The Three Tuns, New York's Flatiron building in miniature, is close by on Silver Street.

61___Park Hill

Reviving the utopian dream of collective living

On the hillside rising up behind Sheffield Station, there are two great, man-made monuments within easy walking distance of each other. One, a three-faceted, needle-like sliver of rising stone with religious detailing, is the Cholera Monument, and it commemorates the deaths of the 402 people who perished of the disease here in 1832. Most were buried in unmarked graves. Only the death of the Master Cutler prompted a pompous, inscribed, horizontal slab of stone.

Walk through Sheaf Valley Park to the north, and you will find a much bigger and less sombre venture altogether: the Park Hill Flats, a giant housing estate consisting of huge, interlocking flanks of multi-story buildings fashioned from concrete, articulated by lattice work, in the Le Corbusier manner, first opened in 1961, which began life as a utopian dream of collective living. That dream died in the 1980s, when the local economy was collapsing, the cost of maintaining the vast structure proved insupportable, and the flats themselves, crime-riddled to a degree, had come to be regarded as a place of last resort.

Thirty years on, and now described as Europe's largest listed structure, the flats are being rebranded, refurbished, and resold to a new generation of believers in the ideals of collective living. Panels of coloured glass brighten those concrete flanks. The plinths of a new sculpture park can be seen from one of the elevated, open-air streets which run, like endless corridors, behind the flats at the backs of the buildings. And, looking out from the front, the views of Sheffield city centre from this elevated standpoint are astonishingly comprehensive – your eye sweeps up from Sheffield Station to the Victorian Town Hall, from the two cathedrals to the Hallamshire Hospital, and then back and beyond until it grazes the moorlands of the Peak District. How close the countryside is from here!

Address Park Hill, S2 | Getting there Park Hill rises up behind Sheffield Station as the train draws in. Leave by the back (tram) exit, turn left, and keep walking for five minutes. | Hours Unrestricted | Tip Take your picnic to the tranquillity of nearby Sheaf Valley Park.

62 Parkwood Springs

Sheffield flung out cinematically

Rutland Road plunges fiercely downhill – watch the cyclists, heads low and facing into the wind. Close to the top, a bridle path, signed to the right, leads you into Parkwood Springs, one of Sheffield's most magnificent hillsides. As you walk east to west, you'll enjoy the sweeping views of the toy town of Sheffield neatly planted down in the valley below - cathedral spire, town hall and all - and beyond. The sunlight plays upon the fields of Derbyshire.

Why does Parkwood Springs feel so embattled though? This hillside, once a wooded deer park, was punished by humans throughout the 20th century. Its central bowl became a huge council waste tip. That area is still bounded by spiked, don't-touch-me fencing. Capped pipes poke up, venting methane gas from all that shallow-concealed, rotting rubbish. The soil is hard-bitten, acidic. Now nature, ever opportunistic, has begun its long fight back. In fact, it is flourishing here once again. New cycle tracks have opened up, and the place is crisscrossed by paths for walkers, who skirt bracken and furze. This is a parkland with a long history - Richard II gave its owner, Sir Thomas de Mounteney, a license to create a deer park here in 1392.

At the western end, you begin the long walk down towards Hillsborough and one of Sheffield's most marvellous cemeteries, Ward's End, cruelly bisected by a railway track, rests on the hillside, which gives its Victorian gravestones an extraordinary, plunging drama. And just beside the track on the southside, a matter of yards from the bridge which you use to cross it, there is a grave memorial that is unlike any other. It belongs to a footballer who plunged to his death while playing football, and who is remembered here with great ceremoniousness. At the foot end of his monument, there is a sculpted football in stone – an unusual site to see!

Address Rutland Road, Sheffield S5 8XB, www.parkwood-springs.org.uk | Getting there
Buses 32, 83/83a, 95/95a from city centre; by car, take A 61 northbound, B 6070, left into Cooks
Wood Road | Hours Unrestricted | Tip Admire the grand façade (1798) of the old Royal
Infirmary building from the bottom of Rutland Road, where part of Ken Loach's terrifying
Threads about Sheffield under nuclear attack was filmed when the building was empty.

63__ The Peace Gardens

Picasso's doves squat on a chimney pot

The Peace Gardens, a miniature recreation area which sits in the shadow of Sheffield's Victorian Town Hall (a great Baroque church called St Paul's once stood on this site), is a place where the dead are remembered, and the living can enjoy a little respite on a bench with a sandwich as they sit part-surrounded by water cascading from a series of giant stone goblets into stepped waterfalls. These cascades were created in memory of the young Sheffield Chartist leader Samuel Holberry who died on the treadmill in York Prison in 1842, aged 28, fighting for fundamental political freedoms. Elsewhere, other memorials are set into walls that back onto Cheney Row on the Town Hall side of the garden, memorialising the military and civilian casualties of war, those who died at Hiroshima, or were killed fighting in the Spanish Civil War.

The most elusive tribute to a man of peace is on the other side of the gardens, and it sits on the edge of a tall-stacked, ribbed Victorian chimney pot on the roof of a building in St Paul's Parade, directly above a hairdressing salon. It is a small flock of like-minded birds, high-polished and sun-reflective, slightly askew to each other, and they are easily missed for two reasons: they are very modest in size, and they compete for our attention on the edge of this chimney pot with a gruesome television aerial. Being Sheffield birds, they are fashioned from flattened polished steel, by a sculptor called Richard Bartle. These birds are three-dimensional versions of Pablo Picasso's dove of peace, a symbol that he drew innumerable times during his lifetime. He even scribbled some on napkins in Sheffield. The 20th century's most talked about artist came to the city in 1950 – he was greeted at Sheffield Midland Station by a well-wisher with a bouquet of flowers – to address the Second World Peace Congress at the City Hall.

Address Pinstone Street, S1 | Getting there 7–10-minute walk from Sheffield Station or Sheffield Interchange up Howard Street, across Arundel Gate, past the Millennium Galleries, along Surrey Street, turning left after the Town Hall | Hours Unrestricted | Tip One of the napkins that Picasso illustrated with a dove of peace is in the archive of the Weston Park Museum. Fragile, it is occasionally on display.

64 Percy Riley Corner

Where the struggle of the miners is remembered

It is often said that history is written by the victors. Where, in or near Sheffield, can you find any reference to the national Miners' Strike of 1984, one of the defining political struggles of the past half-century? Go to the field at Orgreave where the battles took place between miners and police, and you will find not a field any more but the Waverley Estate, a mixed-use development whose name suggests the fantastical remoteness of the novels of Sir Walter Scott. There is no memorial of any kind. In fact, Orgreave as a place with a tangible past barely seems to exist at all. It is little more than a place name at the corner of a road as you quickly pass through to elsewhere. The collieries have gone. The old coking plant has been demolished. All that physically remains by way of evidence that mining occurred in these parts is the odd street name: Coalbrook Avenue, Coalbrook Grove… The Sheffield headquarters of the National Union of Mineworkers has re-opened as a restaurant.

There is one memorial, and you will struggle to spot it. It is a rectangular plaque embedded in the ground beside a tree occasionally hung with fairy lights, at the top of Fargate, in the very centre of the city, overlooked by the tower of Sheffield's Victorian Town Hall. It records the stubborn support offered to miners and their families by a local communist and trade union activist called Percy Riley. The first communist councillor ever to be elected for South Yorkshire, and one of the men who lobbied for the World Peace Congress to be staged in Sheffield in 1950, Riley stood here every day, in good weather and bad, collecting money for the miners. He died after a prolonged bout of illness not long after the strike ended in comprehensive defeat. A cartoon in a local paper once showed him being knighted by 'King' Arthur Scargill, leader of the National Union of Mineworkers.

Address Top of Fargate, a few paces from Sheffield Town Hall, S1 | Getting there
10-minute walk from Sheffield Station up Howard Street, across Arundel Gate, and along
Surrey Street until you find yourself at the top of Fargate | Hours Unrestricted | Tip A little
way down Fargate you will spot the entrance to Chapel Walk, a delightful alleyway. Seek
out Bird's Yard at number 44, a shop full of excellent work by local makers, ranging from
jewellery and clothes to greetings cards.

PERCY RILEY CORNER
DEDICATED TO THE MEMORY OF PERCY RILEY 1920 – 1986
DE UNION AND TENANTS LEADER, TIRELESS WORKER FOR HUMAN RIGHTS AND WORLD PEACE
WHOSE LIFE COMBINED COUNTLESS STRUGGLES FOR A BETTER WORLD.
ING THE WINTER OF 1984 – 1985 PERCY BECAME A WELL KNOWN AND LOVED FIGURE,
OOD DAILY AT THIS SPOT IN ALL WEATHERS COLLECTING IN SUPPORT OF STRIKING
MINERS AND THEIR FAMILIES.

65 Portland Works

All the little mesters under one roof

Even an old factory can spring a surprise. The great, red-brick chimney which dominates the skyline at the centre of the Portland Works used to funnel smoke from a steam engine. Now it's topped by a sprightly looking rowan tree. Five years ago a group of locals saved this remarkable place from destruction. It was created in the 1870s as a fully integrated cutlery factory where all the different 'little mesters' involved in the making of small hand tools – forgers, grinders, finishers – could be brought together in a cluster of workshops with a cobbled courtyard. In 2013, following a citywide campaign, 500 shareholders raised £500,000 to buy the works for the community.

This is the place to which, in 1914, the metallurgist and inventor Harry Brearley brought his new stainless steel to be forged into cutlery. It is also where modernity melds easily with traditional skills. The jewellery-maker works with stainless steel these days. Michael May, fabricator of a pocket knife which has been made in Sheffield for 250 years, has inherited the hand tools of a famous predecessor. There are metalworkers, artists, and even a rug-maker.

Andy Cole, burly and bearded, has worked here for 40 years, and currently specialises in the making of wood chisels. He buys his steel by the ton, from Austria. His workshop, a murky, greasy, dark interior, reeks of oil. Andy sits astride his wooden 'saddle' as you would sit astride the back of any horse – in fact, this way of working is called 'horsing' – leans forward, and offers up a metal blade to the grindstone. Water pours down onto it as the sparks fly furiously. When he is finished, he demonstrates the keenness of the edge by cutting through a sheet of newspaper with a single deft flick. Andy is a productive man when the orders come in. He once made 45,000 steels for pneumatic drills in a single year.

Address Randall Street, S2 4SJ, +44 (0)114 275 9354, www.portlandworks.co.uk, visits@portlandworks.co.uk | Getting there Bus 75, 76, 97 or 98 from High Street or Pinstone Street to London Road/Hill Street, then walk down Hill Street to third on left Randall Street; or car: Randall Street is just off Bramall Lane (A 621), on-street parking | Hours Mon–Fri 9am–5pm | Tip The excellent Harland Cafe is just around the corner at 68 John Street.

66 Queen Cartimandua
Deal-maker with the Romans

Wincobank Hill has been many things in its time. One side of it overlooks an unauthorised housing development that once did its best to scale and tame what was left of that side of the hill. Local activists sued the developers of that estate, and with the money they won, they created a little park, Wincobank Common, on the other side of Jenkin Road, which skirts the hill's western flank.

The soil for the park has been carried up from the valley. Rummage through it with your fingers, and you will find furnace clinker a-plenty with which to grubby your hands. You will also find a monument in the shape of a disc to Cartimandua, Queen of the Brigantes, who once formed an alliance with the Romans. Who was this queen? The name Boudicea lives on to this day. And yet who has ever remembered Queen Cartimandua? Yes, there is a second, equally important, queen of the Ancient Britons, alive at the same time as Boudicea. She was hereditary monarch of Brigantia, a vast territory which stretched north from the Humber to close to the Scottish Borders. The only public record of her presence in the whole of England is to be found on this common in north-east Sheffield, close to that Iron Age fort.

The brain-child of an artist named Ana Ostina, the monument is a low-lying, circular disc of concrete and polished black granite. Around its rim, Cartimandua's name appears, star-crossed lover of a Roman armour-bearer, her second husband Vellocatus. At its centre, there is a star map of the constellations that can be seen in the northern hemisphere.

This common was once a blighted place called Chapman's Tip, a dumping ground for rubbish spewed out by the steel industry down in the Don valley below, complete with vents to let the escaping methane breathe out its worst. Now it is a stretch of close-cropped, levelled parkland, complete with handsome wooden benches.

Address Jenkin Road, Sheffield, S9 | Getting there Bus X 78 to Meadowhall, then a 9-minute walk to the bottom of Jenkin Road; tram to Meadowhall terminus; by car, take A 6109 out of city, then turn left up Jerkin Road, off-street parking on right halfway up | Hours Unrestricted | Tip Enjoy a picnic on one of the benches around the park.

67__Record Collector

Vintage vinyl never stops revolving

Unmissable in its hand-painted, red-and-yellow retro livery, brash and blary as any ripe tomato, the double shopfront onto hilly Fulwood Road in the centre of Broomhill displays a medley of vintage vinyl and press cuttings. The signage screams out the message: *Sheffield's largest independent record store – over 20,000 titles in stock!* Record Collector has been a hub of Sheffield and its music-making since 1978, when Barrie Everard, fresh from a job managing a Virgin record store, first opened for business here. As a young man, he had been sent to a minor public school. Only his passion for popular music saved him from that Alcatraz. Now a bit of a vintage himself, dressed all in black, with only open-toed sandals to keep him cool on a hot afternoon, he happily reminisces beside a counter teetering with cardboard boxes and rock and pop memorabilia. Behind him, stretching back and back into the depths of the shop, there are wall-mounted sleeves of countless long-playing records by the likes of Clapton, Cream, Genesis, and, between the music, other prizes: the presentation made to Barrie when Gomez won the Mercury Prize – Barrie knew them well – or the many black-and-white photographs of John Lydon, Neil Young, Michael Stype and numerous others, once gifted to him by another close friend, Tom Sheehan, one of *Melody Maker*'s staff photographers.

Barrie, eyes serenely closed, pieces together highlights from his almost half a century as a voyeur of, and a participant in, the music scene – that night at Sheffield University Students' Union when David Bowie, soon to make a great splash as Ziggy Stardust, played an entire impassioned set in full kit to an indifferent audience of fewer than 10 in the early hours. Are there really only 20,000 vinyl discs here? More like a hundred thousand, he reassures. Music is Barrie's religion, and this is his church.

Address 233–235 Fulwood Road, S10 3BA, +44 (0)114 266 8493 | Getting there Bus 51, 52 or 52a from Church Street to Broomhill shops, then walk along Fulwood Road; or car: take A57 (Glossop) to Broomhill, Parkers Lane (S10 2SR) and Spooner Road (S10 3BB) car parks | Hours Thu–Sat 10am–5.45pm | Tip Just a few doors down, glance up at the lovely ceramic cartouche embedded into the broken pediment above the door of the Fox and Duck. This delightfully colourful nursery-rhyme chase is almost – almost – the equal of a Luca della Robbia.

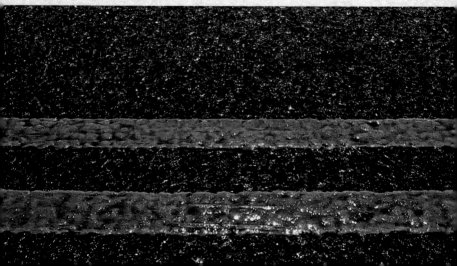

68 __Redmires Training Camp

Where local boys prepared for the Somme

The area of woodland behind the Sportsman public house at Lodge Moor, almost abutting the wild moorlands of the Peak District, harbours secrets to tempt any curious urban archaeologist. These woods, grown up since the 1950s, were once the site of Redmires Training Camp, which was set up to prepare the Sheffield City Battalion for the miseries of battle in France during World War I. The volunteers, all professional men (teachers, solicitors, cutlers) who had responded to the call to join Kitchener's Army, were called to the Somme in 1916 and suffered terrible casualties. Their slightly elevated status caused the battalion to be named the 'coffee and bun' boys. During that war, the camp expanded to become an internment camp for enemy aliens. During World War II, the camp was re-used, often with the aid of scavenged materials. At war's end, farmers and others scavenged all over again. The sole surviving example of the buildings that once stood here is the World War I hut behind the pub.

There is still much to be found amongst the snaggly, briary undergrowth. Picking about this woodland needs to be undertaken with care. No child should go unaccompanied. Though the huts themselves are long gone, there are brick, rectangular footings of buildings, with low flights of steps leading up to nowhere, or fragments of ceramic pipe. Your toe caps (always wear boots in these woods) impact against what look like giant metal staples driven into the ground – these would have kept coils of barbed-wire fencing in place. In the field directly to the west, you happen upon a ghost of a circle in the grass, with a darkened centre. Its greenness is quite different from what surrounds it. This is the spot where the uniforms of the prisoners of war were burnt at the end of hostilities. Scuff at the soil with your boot. You might turn up a button or a scrap of webbing.

Address The woods behind the Sportsman, Redmires Road, S10 | **Getting there** Bus 51 from High Street to Lodge Moor terminus, then walk along Redmires Road to take public footpath at side of Sportsman onto playing field next to the woods; train to Sheffield station; or car: take A 57 (Glossop) from city centre, turn left at Crosspool onto Sandygate Road, and continue along Redmires Road, on-street parking | **Hours** Unrestricted | **Tip** The Sportsman displays good walking boots on a windowsill for sale at knock-down prices.

69 Ringinglow Roundhouse

Practising the art of snooping in every direction

It is a long, hard, steady climb up the arrow-straight toll road west out of Sheffield to Ringinglow. Perhaps this road is a little too straight and speed-encouraging. A local boxing hero, Prince Naseem, once seriously injured a man by thundering along it at 90 miles an hour as a boast, and was imprisoned for the misdemeanour. Just five miles out of the city centre – an ancient milestone tells you so – you have shucked off most of human civilisation, and you are on your way to the high, hard-bitten, wind-scoured moorlands of the Peaks.

But just before you reach that point, you arrive at the 18th-century Ringinglow Roundhouse, the most magnificent of many toll houses in the Sheffield of then or now. (Across from the Roundhouse sits the Norfolk Arms, a fine, early-Victorian building, where thirsts can be slaked.) Often the subject of paintings, this toll house rises three storeys. Its appearance vaguely nodding in the direction of a church or some castle's outbuilding (its own outbuildings are in fact castellated), this wonderful gobbet of no-holds-barred utility melded with just a dab of fancifulness. It has the look of an octagonal pepper pot, with two tiers of steeply arched window apertures (not all are in fact windows) on each of its eight sides, and a roof like a party hat, topped by an octagonal chimney. The third-storey walls feature blind shamrock shapes. The walls are a rough-rendered grey-brown, which turns, like some trick, surprisingly pinkish at dusk. Why so many all-seeing eyes? Watchfulness was the order of the day. Three roads converged at this point, and the man in the toll house needed to keep a careful eye on every one of them to ensure that traffic did not slip through, unnoticed, without paying the levy. These days, cycling hospital consultants might flash by, harmlessly enough, in their Lycra strip, often in tight packs.

Never underestimate the speed of rivalrous medics.

Address Ringinglow Road, Ringinglow, S11 7TS | **Getting there** Bus 4 (limited service) from Sheffield Interchange; or car: take A625 (Ecclesall Road) south-west out of city until it meets the Ringinglow Road, on-street parking | **Tip** Five minutes' walk from here, along Fulwood Lane, is the Mayfield Alpacas Animal Park, where the entire family can cosy up to a llama (www.mayfieldanimalpark.co.uk).

70_ The Rivelin Valley Trail

The beautiful afterlife of industry

The monumental statue of Ebenezer Elliott, the poet of 19th-century Sheffield who thundered against the iniquities of central government taxation in his Corn Law Rhymes, sits raised up, rather surprisingly, not on some pompous, throne-aspiring chair, but on a rock in Weston Park, just beside the oldest buildings of Sheffield University. Local historians have speculated that this rock was modelled on one in the Rivelin Valley, which is now one of Sheffield's most delightful urban-cum-pastoral trails.

The Rivelin Trail is in a narrow, deep-set valley, and it tells the story of Sheffield's industrial success in the 18th century and before. That success depended upon the harnessing of the power of water, which Sheffield always possessed in great abundance thanks to the five rivers which flow down to it from the moorlands of the Peak District to the west. How to successfully harness this water in the service of industry? The Rivelin Valley Trail shows us how, and that demonstration takes place down the entire length of a secretive valley of great beauty, with a slender and elegant pack-horse bridge at its western end. As you proceed from the Coppice Wheel Pool downstream towards Malin Bridge and the city you'll find stepping stones over which you can trip nimbly if you have the nerve and the balance (there are also means of avoiding them), twisty paths beneath overhanging trees, and a river whose muscular force would once have been diverted to enable, for example, a great millstone to turn in order to make keen the edge of a blade. That industry has all gone from here, of course, and what remains is its ghostly presence as a lovely public amenity – remnants of sluice gates, for example. This linear park serves as a posthumous reminder of how, thanks to human ingenuity, nature and industry were able to work in close and successful collaboration.

Address Rivelin Valley, S6 | Getting there To begin your walk upstream, drive to the junction of Rivelin Valley Road (A 6101) with the Manchester Road (A 57) and park at the Rails Road car park, or, downstream, join the Rivelin Valley Road at Malin Bridge; or tram to Malin Bridge | Hours Unrestricted | Tip At the Malin Bridge end of the trail there's a lovely splash pool for children.

71__The River Don Engine
The muscular force of steam power

This is the largest and most powerful working steam engine in the country, and it is difficult to encompass in mere words its almost overwhelming, muscularly physical presence within the gallery that it occupies, soaring ceiling-high, its huge footings contained within a deep-sunken well, surrounded by drums of grease. Davy Bros of Sheffield made this 400-ton, 12,000-horse-power machine, tricked out to impress in its green-and-red livery, in 1905. The size of its nuts and bolts would put a Cyclops' fist to shame, and its three gleaming silver pistons look as smoothly articulated as some super-subtle robot's. When, having turned in one direction, they idle a little while before going into reverse, it looks like the trickery of some marvellous circus performance – a contortionist's perhaps.

The accompanying low, drum-like boom, which increases in volume as the engine gains speed, and the steady upward trickle of drifting steam, turn the whole experience a touch more Hogwartish. The very ground beneath your feet begins to vibrate. Yes, what is going on here when it works – and it does so for marvelling visitors and their unusually still and speechless children several times a day because its new gas boiler was replaced as recently 2016 – is a recreation of pure theatre in order to remind us all of the history of this magnificent piece of mechanical engineering, and all the work it did when it drove the rolling mill at the River Don Engine Works.

Its purpose? Rolling out armour plate for battleships. The first-one-way-and-then-the-other action is to do with the fact that the metal had to go back and forth so that it could be flattened to exactly the right thickness at exactly the right speed – rather as you take a rolling pin to a slab of pastry. The engine stayed in service with Cammell Laird for 50 years, and was finally retired from the front line in 1978.

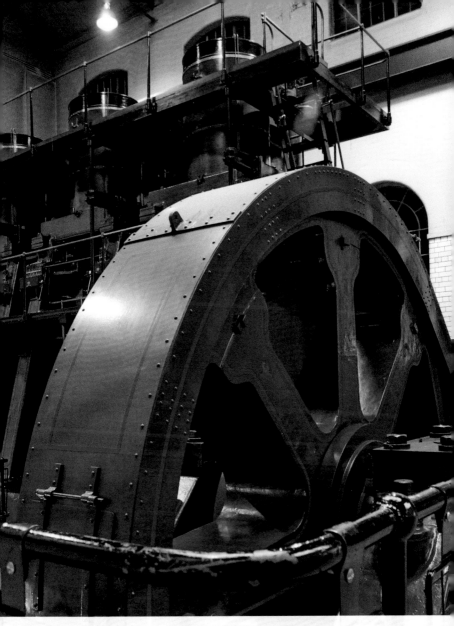

Address Kelham Island Museum, Alma Street, S3 8RY, +44 (0)114 272 2106, www.simt.co.uk, ask@simt.co.uk | Getting there Bus 7, 8 or 8a from Arundel Gate to Nursery Street (opposite Harlequin pub); cross the river and walk along the river path to Kelham; or tram to Shalesmoor, cross the road and walk down Green Lane and Alma Street; or car: Kelham Island Museum is signed off the A 61 inner relief road, access via Alma Street, free visitor parking. | Hours Tue – Sun 10am – 4pm | Tip Try the excellent salmon fishcakes at the Grind Cafe just a short walk away.

72 Royal Exchange Buildings

Just a whiff of Amsterdam beside the River Don

Before you foot-slog up Waingate into the centre of Sheffield, you have to cross Lady's Bridge, the most ancient fording point of the River Don. Stare down at the bridge's foundations and you'll see evidence of earlier structures – the bridge was first created in the Middle Ages, and stood close to Sheffield Castle, which was demolished at the end of England's Civil War as a punishment for its commander's support of the Royalist cause. Once this river was as polluted as hell's mouth – the river ran pink or mauve when the paper mill upstream opted for a vivid choice of hue. Now wild flowers grow on its banks, and fish nudge at the surface. The shallow water positively babbles. The Exchange Brewery once overlooked this bridge – a plaque makes that clear – so that travellers into town by tram or bus caught the sweet smell of fermenting hops in the nostrils. These days, if you stand beside the site of the old brewery and look upriver about 100 metres, you can spot a launching point for a kayak or a canoe.

Directly across from the bridge are the Royal Exchange Buildings, which rank amongst Sheffield's most wonderfully fanciful architectural structures, with stepped gabling reminiscent of some canal-side scene in Amsterdam. The variegated colours of the brickwork are a delight too: from an orangey-pink to a mellow brown. Walk in the building's shadow along the river, and you see how pleasingly odd it all is: a lovely, tall square structure with long, stretched windows and towering chimneys rising up at its back like something created for Old Mother Hubbard. A variety of inhabitants have passed through, some quite as colourful as the buildings themselves. They were built around 1900 for a vet and animal breeder called John Henry Bryers. A Home for Lost Dogs opened in July of that same year. Sick horses lodged at the rear. Even elephants have been welcomed.

Address 8 Lady's Bridge, S3 8GA | Getting there 20-minute walk from Sheffield Interchange. Walk through bus station to end of Pond Street, which becomes hilly Flat Street. Carry on into Fitzalan Square and down through Haymarket towards Lady's Bridge. The Royal Exchange buildings face the bridge on the right. | Hours Unrestricted | Tip The Five Weirs Walk begins at Lady's Bridge (www.fiveweirs.co.uk).

73 Royal Victoria Station Hotel

Wilde, Pavlova and a chorus line of flappers

The Royal Victoria Station Hotel. Sheffield. Why say more? There was no other hotel in Sheffield when Oscar Wilde telegraphed his congratulations to the actress Lily Langtry from this address on 22 January, 1884 for having taken America by storm in her role as Lady Ormonde in *Peril*.

The hotel, which opened in 1862, was created to serve the new Yorkshire and Lincolnshire Railway, and to this day it smacks of excess. It was described as a first-class hotel for families and gentlemen, complete with private apartments and suites of rooms, and it was under the direct management of the Manchester, Sheffield & Lincolnshire Railway Company. Trains drew up along a platform outside the door. A hotel porter was in attendance upon all trains. As that railway had to be carried along an immense, curving viaduct to avoid the River Don, the hotel itself had to be painstakingly raised up on a tall plinth, which is where it sits to this day, as if it were some Renaissance palazzo fearful of invaders.

Royalty, aristocrats, flappers, dancers – Pavlova, for example – washed in and out. Its glittery ballroom, which boasts a stuccoed ceiling insured for £3 million, has a minstrels' gallery at one end. When King Edward VII and Queen Alexandra sat down to dinner at the hotel on 7 July, 1905 at the invitation of The Lord Mayor and Members of the Executive Committee, they were served the following: a spring soup described as Creme a la Windsor, Boiled Turbot with Duglere Sauce, Foie-Gras, Roast Sirloin of Beef with trimmings, Roast Duckling, Souffle Pudding, Raspberry Cream Ice and a final course described as Dessert. And all washed down with Sherry, Berncastler Doctor, Louis Roederer-Ex.Dry, 1893.

Address Victoria Station Road, S4 7YE, +44 (0)114 276 8822, www.cpsheffield.co.uk, stay@cpsheffield.co.uk | **Getting there** 10-minute walk from Sheffield Station via Park Square roundabout. Take fifth exit signposted Victoria Quays. Turn right at first set of traffic lights. Entrance to the hotel drive is on your immediate left. | **Hours** Daily 10am–5pm, but call in advance of visit | **Tip** Admire the magnificent war memorial just outside the hotel's entrance.

74__ The Ruskin Collection

Handing beauty on to the working man

John Ruskin, wealthy Victorian aesthetician, art critic, painter, amateur botanist and a man with a social conscience, had great admiration for the skills of the craftsmen of Sheffield. He also wanted to teach those locals – the knife grinder, the scythe maker, the worker who toiled for long hours at the forge in blistering heat – how to appreciate the beauty of fine-made things. This wish culminated in the creation of a museum, which included not only man-made objects such as a window moulding from a Venetian palazzo, but natural things too: a piece of quartz, an oak leaf, a peacock feather.

He established that museum in 1875, in a remote rural spot called Walkley overlooking the beautiful Rivelin Valley, a place with views 'suggestive of the Alps', Ruskin wrote. Ruskin wanted the museum to be out in the countryside so that its visitors would have some respite from the poor air of what had already become one of the great, smoke-choked powerhouses of Victorian England. He stuffed it to the brim with objects. Its opening hours were unusually long. A former pupil, Henry Swan, became its first curator. That collection of objects – paintings (including many of Ruskin's own), prints, books, manuscripts, plaster casts from buildings, samples of minerals and much else – still remains in Sheffield, in an intimate gallery in the city centre. The corner close to the entrance where the bust of Ruskin sits feels a little like someone's Victorian parlour. Feel free to poke around, pulling out drawers of specimens. On the end wall, there is a painting of Saint Mark's Basilica in Venice, painted by John Bunney.

Ruskin wanted to transport the people of Sheffield elsewhere, and to quicken their own spirit of inventiveness. A young local knife grinder called Joseph Creswick, then in poor health, was so inspired by his visit to the museum that he became a successful portrait sculptor.

Address Millennium Gallery, Arundel Gate, S1 2PP, www.museums-sheffield.org.uk/
museums/millennium-gallery/exhibitions/current/ruskin-collection | **Getting there** Short
walk from Sheffield station | **Hours** Tue–Sat 10am–5pm, Sun 11am–4pm | **Tip** A plaque
at 381 South Road, Walkley, commemorates the site of the original museum.

75 _ Sandygate

The oldest football ground in continuous use

Much of the early history of the global game we know as football was written in Sheffield. The world's oldest clubs are Sheffield F.C. (1857) and Hallam F.C. (1860), both still thriving non-league sides. The first football rule book was written in Sheffield, in 1858, differentiating the game from rugby and other sports. And the most sacred patch of footballing turf is Sandygate, to the west of the city, home of Hallam F.C. This sloping patch of ground, sited above the snow line, part bounded by a long Victorian stone wall, and within easy reach of open moorland, is the oldest ground in continuous use as a football pitch in the world. Sandygate, once at the edge of nowhere, was where it began.

Hallam F.C. is a modest affair. The single stand seats 250, and the average attendance at a home match is 150. Tickets on a Saturday cost £5. Those first players would have been employees of the club's creator, John Charles Shaw, a supplier of stationery to solicitors. The reason for the game's creation was simple and sensible. Cricket was played here before football elbowed it aside, and it was impossible to play cricket in the winter months. Let football keep the men occupied instead. They would have changed into their heavy flannelette shirts, and pulled on their hob-nailed boots, in the Plough, the pub which is still visible directly across from the entrance to the ground. In 1857, there were no other teams to play against, so Sheffield F.C. played against themselves – the single against the married, for example. Then Hallam F.C. came along, and that annual derby between the two Sheffield clubs continues to this day.

That Sheffield Rule Book changed everything. It stipulated a crossbar for the goal mouth, flags, a kick-off, penalties, fouls; no handling of the ball; the length of the game to be set at 90 minutes. The modern game of football was made in Sheffield.

Address Sandygate Road, S10 5SE, +44 (0)114 230 9484, www.hallamfc.co.uk, theclub@hallamfc.co.uk | **Getting there** Bus 51 from High Street to Sandygate Road, next to Hallam F.C. (junction with Carsick Hill Road); or car: take A 57 (Glossop) and then left onto Sandygate Road at Crosspool, free on-site parking | **Hours** Tue & Wed 6–11pm, Sat noon–11pm | **Tip** Scenes from *When Saturday Comes*, starring Sheffield's own Sean Bean, were filmed here. The boots Bean wore when he scored the winning goal are in Legends of the Lane Museum at Bramall Lane. They are surprisingly small.

76_Scaling the Norman Fort
Keeping the marauders at bay

Expect the company of sheep when in the borough of Greater Shef-field. And especially so in the graveyard of St Nicholas at High Brad-field, an ancient village that hangs high above the Loxley Valley to the north-west of the city. This fine medieval church, finically crock-eted and gargoyled, hosts an annual festival of classical music in June which has welcomed Julian Lloyd Webber, the Ensemble Berlin, and Sheffield's very own Lindsay String Quartet. The Tour de France passed through this hilliest of hilly villages in 2014, and you can still see the welcoming graffiti, blazoned in yellow, on the road down which the packs of blurry legs thundered: *ALLEZ! ALLEZ! Vroom, Vroom, Froome!* The village pub, The Old Horns Inn, which must be visited for the magnificent, flung-out prospect of the valley you can enjoy in its child-friendly picnic garden, still has a yellow bike hung above its stone-pedimented door.

Push through the gate into the cemetery, with its fine array of Victorian funerary monuments, and you will likely meet, in their favourite shady nook of a high-raised mound beneath a tree, a wel-coming sheep or two, nudging or nuzzling at you. But don't take them with you as you proceed beyond the cemetery, and then throw a right towards what has already been signposted as Bailey Hill. After a very short uphill walk, you'll come upon an extraordinary scene, half hid-den by trees: an enormous, towering earth mound, once created by human hands, which doughty beeches and smaller oaks are aspiring to climb and to subjugate, encircled by a ditch and a partially dilap-idated drystone wall. Scrabbling up its side to the summit is tough going, but there's a snaky, slippery route for those wearing good, grippy boots. This is the great remnant of one of Yorkshire's finest motte-and-bailey forts, set down here to keep out the marauders from the northerly kingdom of Northumbria.

Address High Bradfield, S6 | Getting there Bus 61 or 62 from Arundel Gate to High Bradfield, then follow the public footpath at the side of the church to the the fort on Bailey Hill; or car: take A 61 North B 6076, on-street parking in the village | Hours Unrestricted | Tip The Old Horns Inn at the entrance to the village has an especially panoramic garden on the hillside directly below the pub, complete with a colourful bouncy castle for children of all ages.

77__Sewer Gas Destructor Lamp

Which flares up brightest at Christmas

Sometimes a green street light on a fairly narrow, rising hogsback, overlooking allotments that spill down a hillside, and almost canopied by hazel, ash, sycamore and beech, can be much more than it seems. Here is an elegant object which deals, quite deftly, with an inelegant problem. This is the finest remaining example in Sheffield of a light that was created to deal with the terrible problem of the random escape of sewage gas.

Sheffield was a great industrialised city built on hills, and hilliness brought complications. Noxious, inflammable gases were inclined to get trapped in small quantities. Fumes escaped. Workers were at perpetual risk of an explosion. Residents, understandably enough, turned up their noses. This lamp, which burns with a particularly hot flame, was invented and patented in 1895 by Joseph Edmund Webb of Birmingham, and Sheffield put in an order for 84 of them – a larger quantity than any other city. They were all installed between 1915 and 1935. Joseph Webb's Sewage Gas Destructor Lamp served a dual purpose: it burnt off both the sewage gases and the town gases, and it served as a street light too – as it continues to do so until this day. Only two of them are still in full working order.

The lamp is part tight-pinched into a long stretch of ancient wall topped by characteristic triangular coping. The surface of the circular column which rises to support the chamber – once gas-lit – is fluted. Its hinged top is capped by a spiked coronet of sorts. The glass is toughened, and looks slightly smoggy, as if it is dolefully reminiscing about the days before the Clean Air Acts came into force. The lamp's long, thin horizontal arms seem to be directing traffic. It burns brightest at Christmas, when the fortunate of Sheffield live high on the hog.

Address Brincliffe Edge Road, S11 | Getting there Bus 81, 82 or 88 from Leopold Street to Ecclesall Road at top of Brincliffe Edge Road; or car: take A 625 from city centre, on-street parking around Brincliffe Edge Road | Hours Unrestricted | Tip The very first flood-lit football match was played in Sheffield, on 14 October, 1878, at Bramall Lane, still the home ground of Sheffield United.

78__Sharrow Vale Road

A most distinctively local shopping street

One of the best ways to enjoy what Sharrow Vale Road has to offer is to walk down it from the Hunter's Bar roundabout, where you will spot a 19th-century toll gate marooned in the middle of the road, part-hidden amongst trees and shrubs. This may be the only toll gate in England with its own Twitter account. The road itself twists a little as you descend a gentle hill. Noisy kids are racing around the playground of the primary school just across from the shops. It's a modest enough affair of two-storey Victorian terracing, part houses, part shops, often interrupted by small cobbled gennels, but it sparks into life immediately as you enter it: lazily appealing bouzouki music is oozing out from the Greedy Greek Deli close to the corner. Bright-shining blue tables are out on the pavement, ready to be heaped high with souvlaki.

There is a lot of spilling out of goods onto pavements down this street: boots displayed on a table outside the shoe shop; brooms standing to attention at the hardware store; flowers at the Brookhouse florist; veg, scruffy with soil, at Barra Organics. This is one of Sheffield's finest and most distinctive shopping streets. There are no chains here. Every shop offers something new, from the hardware store and the excellent fish shop, to Seven Hills Bakery and the Porter Brook Delicatessen, where Nicky from the Black Country and her partner Nick from Sheffield mull over the reasons for the street's success. As you listen, it is possible to sample a few slivers of some of their 60 distinctive cheeses. A recent arrival is a cow's cheese called Stanage Millstone from Hathersage in the Peak District, which comes in the shape of a tiny millstone. There are more than 50 independent businesses on this street, and there is a general spirit of sharing; of cooperative, community endeavour. This is a high street sparky as they used to be.

Address Sharrow Vale Road, S11 | Getting there Bus 81, 82, 83, 83a or 88 from Leopold
Street to Ecclesall Road near Hickmott Road, then walk down Hickmott Road to Sharrow
Vale Road; or car: located just off A 625 – at Hunter's Bar Roundabout, turn onto Sharrow
Vale Road, on-street parking | Hours Unrestricted | Tip The Lescar Hotel at 303 Sharrow
Vale Road boasts a fine, 1930s interior and sells good ale. It also hosts regular comedy nights.

79 __ The Sheffield Assay Office
Where precious stuff gets bicycled in

The Sheffield Assay Office is tucked away on an unprepossessing industrial estate near a dog-racing track in a fairly unfashionable part of the city, as if wanting to keep schtum about itself. Once inside, you can understand why. They bring the stuff here on bikes, in rucksacks, or in secure armoured vehicles, objects fashioned in such precious metals as silver, gold, platinum or palladium, for testing and hallmarking.

Assaying has been going on in Sheffield since 1773, set up by an Act of Parliament – this is one of only four such places in the country – and what happens here represents one of the oldest forms of consumer protection. It's also very good for the jeweller, silversmith or cutler because it gives the objects registered and authenticated in this place, often made by the hand of an individual like you or me, gravitas, value, the hallmark of quality and authenticity. It's also a legal requirement if the object exceeds a certain weight.

A tour of the Assay Office enables you to see part of the rolling display of their own collections of about 1,000 objects of jewellery, tableware and cutlery, many of them by Sheffield designer-makers; consult the library where you can sit in a chair fashioned from Japanese oak whose back has been stamped with a rose (the hallmark of Sheffield); and, most exciting of all, see how it all happens on the checking floor itself and, beyond that, in the laboratory. It's fiddly, painstaking work testing and hallmarking objects as tiny as some of the ones here. You need a special kind of indented punch to get round to the inside edge of a ring, for example. Unsurprisingly, some of the punches themselves are enormously valuable – imagine the criminal mayhem let loose if they were lost or stolen. So their custodian, peering down his microscope, works inside a not-so-benign-looking metal cage of sorts…

Address Guardians Hall, 2 Beulah Road, S6 2AN, +44 (0)114 231 2121, www.assayoffice.co.uk, info@assayoffice.co.uk | Getting there Bus 7, 7a, 8, 8a, 85 or 86 from Arundel Gate to Penistone Road (Hillsborough Leisure Centre stop); tram to Hillsborough Park, then cross road, walk through park, down Broughton Road and then across Penistone Road; or car: take A 61 (Barnsley), on-site parking | Hours Mon–Fri 8.30am–4.30pm | Tip The magnificently monumental Ward's End Cemetery, hillside-perched, and part-hidden amongst trees, is 10 minutes' walk from here.

80 Sheffield City Hall

Where John Lennon might have met Ziggy Stardust

This elegant civic hall of the early 1930s, neither too big nor too small, and as pleasingly oval in its shape as any well sucked boiled sweet, is crowded with the ghosts of all those who have entertained audiences here, from Gene Pitney to Roy Orbison, from Billy J. Kramer and the Dakotas to Johnny Kidd and the Pirates, from the Searchers to the Hollies, from Bob Dylan to the Beatles, from Led Zeppelin to Ziggy Stardust. But the history of ever-shifting tastes in popular music is just a part of what has gone on in this place. Contentious political meetings have happened here too. When Oswald Mosley addressed his Blackshirts in the 1930s, an angry crowd of 15,000 anti-fascist demonstrators bayed for blood outside. And down in the basement there is a glamorous ballroom where local hearts have been won and lost over flights of nifty footwork.

Was the place at its most alive in the 1960s? This was the big, open stage where up-and-coming groups – local and national – honed their acts. The young Joe Cocker, a local gas fitter when he was not deep into his squirmy, air-guitar-thrashing role as England's greatest soul singer to come, got his first big break here in 1963, as a support act to the Rolling Stones. Until that moment he had been roaring around the pubs of Sheffield under the stage name of Vance Arnold, with his group the Avengers. The Liverpool Sound made a splash with Gerry Marsden and the Pacemakers. And then Bob Dylan came, in 1965, spindly, intense, lean as a straw, preying on his microphone, in a leather jacket whose sleeves looked a mite too short for him. Wafts from the harmonica. A fierce, jangling guitar sound – he was hitting those steel strings so hard. It was the words that counted, the mesmerising words. Sam Wanamaker captured precious minutes from that concert in Sheffield, on stage and off, in a great documentary called *Don't Look Back*.

Address Barker's Pool, S1 2JA, +44 (0)114 278 9789, www.sheffieldcityhall.co.uk, info@sheffieldcityhall.co.uk | Getting there 15-minute walk from Sheffield Interchange, 1 minute from Sheffield Town Hall | Tip Admire the 90-feet-tall war memorial in Barker's Pool directly outside the hall. It was unveiled in 1925.

81 The Sheffield Simplex

Bespoke luxury fit for the Romanovs

Sheffield's history as a maker of luxury cars was brief and distinctive, and gleaming examples of two of the finest – the Charron-Laycock (known locally as the 'doctor's car' because it was said that only doctors could possibly afford the £500 that it cost to purchase one in the 1920s) and the Sheffield Simplex – can be found in the Charlesworth Transport Gallery. This Simplex in Sheffield, a prototype of 1920, is one of only three examples to survive in the world, and it takes part in rallies to this day. Around 1,500 cars were manufactured at the Simplex Motor Works, Tinsley, between 1907 and 1920. This model, which was touted as a rival in luxury and elegance to the Rolls-Royce, was a victim of its own luxuriousness. Custom-made, it cost far too much to assemble, and it went out of production after 16 years in 1922.

The British Association's Handbook of 1910 is quite boastful about the car and its provenance: 'The Sheffield Simplex Motor Car is well known for its high quality of design and manufacture. The Company undoubtedly find it a great advantage to have their works in the centre of the special steel manufacturing district, as this gives them facilities… which they could not command if they were not immediately in touch with the recent developments of steel manufacture.' Many agreed – including the Tsar of Russia, who bought several. You might well have seen one parked outside the Winter Palace in St Petersburg.

The elegance and swagger of this long, spoke-wheeled four-seater – its bonnet is barrel-vaulted, its black hood retractable, its colour a fetching racing green, and its starter motor electric – are undeniable, and it looks in such good condition because this particular car has lived a very cosseted life. For years it was owned by Earl Fitzwilliam, a local landowner, and it was kept under cover in his stables in Ireland.

Address Charlesworth Transport Gallery, Kelham Island Museum, Alma Street, S3 BRY, +44 (0)114 272 2106, www.simt.co.uk, ask@simt.co.uk | Getting there Bus 7, 8 or 8a from Arundel Gate to Nursery Street (opposite Harlequin pub), cross river and walk along river path to Kelham; tram to Shalesmoor, cross road and walk down Green Lane and Alma Street; or car: Kelham Island Museum is signed off the A 61 inner relief road, access via Alma Street, free visitor parking | Hours Tue–Sun 10am–4pm | Tip Don't miss the astonishing Bessemer Convertor, hanging in the air like a giant, black, armour-plated double egg cup, directly outside the museum.

82_ The Sheffield Tap

Idling luxuriousness beside Platform 1

No one should bid a fond farewell to Sheffield station without sampling a pint of one of the many craft beers, local, national or international, available at the Sheffield Tap, the city's most idlingly luxurious of refurbished Edwardian interiors. A full listing for the discerningly thirsty is chalked up on a slate board in the first bar, and on a regular day you might enjoy a pint of I Love U Will U Marry Me from the Thornbridge Brewing Company or a Vermont Tea Party from Siren Craft.

Three generously long bars – friezes of ornate wall tiles face a rich mahogany counter – look out towards the agitated goings-on of Platform 1, so that as you drink, cosseted by red leather armchairs or banquettes, illuminated by a chandelier here or a Tiffany lamp there, you can watch the trains, in their colourful liveries, nosing sleekly in and out, whilst at the same time keeping half an ear cocked for the announcement of your journey of destiny. The most gorgeously tricked-out of the three platform-facing interiors (there are also little snugs at the back for those who might wish to indulge in a less public liaison) is the farthest one from the entrance, so don't settle too readily for the first two. This one is bourgeois visual panache writ large: white tiling smothers the walls. Drinkers huddle around a huge fireplace. This last bar also proudly shows off various beers in the making in huge, gleaming, copper-clad, drum-like fermentation tanks – courtesy of the Sheffield Tap's own, on-site micro-brewery, the Tapped Brew Company.

The Tap first opened for business in the Edwardian era, when the station itself was young. It fell into disrepair, and was saved from dereliction in 2008. Now the Dining and Refreshment Rooms which were built to serve first-class passengers only can be enjoyed by many more than just the privileged few.

Address 1b, Sheffield Station, Sheaf Street, S1 2BP, +44 (0)114 273 7558, www.sheffieldtap.com | Getting there Walk out of the station and turn right, and the entrance to the Tap is just around the corner | Hours Sun–Thu 11am–11pm, Fri & Sat 10am–midnight | Tip If you leave the station by the back exit in the direction of the tram and walk a little way uphill, you will come across an amphitheatre. Its regular programme of events includes AmphiFest, an annual community festival held over two days on the first weekend in June, open-air film screenings, and touring productions of Shakespeare courtesy of Handlebards.

83 The Sheffield Year Knife

A bravura wonder in two thousand blades

Sheffield has been celebrated for its handmade tools – and especially its knives – since at least the 12th century, but sometimes a particular example seems to surpass all others by the sheer virtuoso bravura of its making. The Sheffield Year Knife takes pride of place in Sheffield's Ken Hawley Collection, the most comprehensive gathering of handmade tools in the world. No other knife possesses quite so many individual blades. When first made in 1821, it was created to be an object of wonder in the new showrooms of Joseph Rodgers in Norfolk Street, and it was said to have had 1,821 blades. More would be added in the coming years: blades for the coronation of Queen Elizabeth II in 1952, for example. The final blade was added in the year 2000, in celebration of the millennium, and the knife is now said to possess 2,000 blades. If you had days to spare, you could stand patiently by and count them, one by one. This knife was therefore being worked on, magnified, made to seem ever more outrageously self-preening, by a variety of master knife-makers over a period of almost 200 years.

And now it sits amongst giant examples of spanners, scissors and garden shears made for trade fairs, in its own glazed wooden cabinet, looking more like an object of religious devotion, ripe for contemplation, than a mere knife, and it sits on a four-footed, gilded plinth, like a cross between a crucifix and an exotic Amazonian head dress. The blades seem to spin out like fireworks from all directions of the compass. Many of the blades are in fact different tools of one kind or another – penknives, even outrageously exotic ones such as this one, have always needed to be useful. There is a corkscrew, a file, a button hook, a saw. Some blades are straight, others curved. The top two blades were made by Stan Shaw, a celebrated 'little mester' of our own day.

Address The Hawley Collection, Kelham Island Museum, Alma Street, S3 8RY, +44 (0)114 201 0770, www.hawleytoolcollection.com, ask@simt.co.uk | Getting there Bus 7, 8 or 8a from Arundel Gate to Nursery Street (opposite Harlequin pub), then cross the river and walk along the river path to Kelham; tram to Shalesmoor, then cross road and walk down Green Lane and Alma Street; on-street parking | Hours Tue–Sun 10am–4pm | Tip Look out for a kingfisher in the mill race outside the museum.

84_ Shepherd Wheel

Walking from city park to open countryside

Sheffield once had a reputation for being so smog-choked by industry that you could barely see your hand in front of your face. Nowadays it is shockingly green. The city has more parkland and ancient woodland than any other European city of a comparable size. You can walk from the heart of the city, through a linked network of linear parks, until you reach open countryside.

Begin at Hunter's Bar, where you join Endcliffe Park. This is the Porter Valley, and as you walk up through the park, Porter Brook, sometimes raging, at other times sleepily sinuous keeps you company (try crossing it by stepping stones if you are nimble of foot). The brook, canopied by trees, looks surprisingly modest in breadth and muscular power, but this modesty is deceptive. As you walk through this narrowing, ever more steep-sided valley, you see repeated evidence of how the power of the water from this brook has been harnessed by man in the interests of local industry. Look out for the goits which diverted water into mill ponds; look out for the mill ponds themselves. There are also monuments to seek out as you go – a sad statue of Queen Victoria close to the entrance to the park, for example, disrespectfully hidden amongst trees, verdigrised, and much shat upon by ignorant birds. Or a stone memorial, on rising ground, to the loss of American lives. A USAAF bomber came down at this exact spot on 22 February, 1944, causing the loss of 10 men.

Crossing a small road, you come to Whiteley Woods. Here you will find a grouping of small and ancient buildings, a mill pond, and, attached to the side of a cutler's finishing shop, with water pouring into it from the pond, the great Shepherd Wheel which, when it rotated in its slow-paced way – as it is doing today – provided the power to turn the grindstones which were used inside. There were once 20 such wheels down this valley.

Address Hangingwater Road, S11 2YE, +44 (0)114 272 2106, ask@simt.co.uk | Getting there Bus 81, 82, 83, 83a or 88 from Leopold Street to top of Ecclesall Road just before Hunter's Bar roundabout; or car: take A 625, on-street parking | Hours Unrestricted | Tip Close to the park's entrance is Trinity United Reformed Church, a remarkable concrete brutalist church of 1971, set into the gaping mouth of an old quarry.

85__ The Showroom

The most versatile of indie cinemas

Some of Sheffield's finest built structures, whether Georgian or Victorian, frequently reinvent themselves. The stylish, two-storey art deco building in black and cream faience which projects itself out from the junction of Paternoster Row and Shoreham Street like a snub-nosed ship's prow, houses the Showroom, Sheffield's most versatile indie cinema. It hasn't always been a cinema. Kenning's first opened the building in 1937 as a garage and car showroom, and the hefty lift once used to raise cars up to the second storey is still in place. Now the building, which has been showing films since the 1990s, sits in the middle of Sheffield's Creative Industries quarter, and it houses four cinemas with memorably strange audience capacities (one can take a maximum of 107, another 282), and a cafe bar which offers gourmet veggie evenings (today's midday, front-of-counter offerings include wasabi peas at £1.25 a portion, or a slice of millionaire shortbread for a mere £1.95). At the back of the cinema complex there is the Showroom Workstation, which can be hired out for conferences or rented by small creatives – designers, publicists, etc. Directly behind the Workstation are recording studios, including Red Tape Studios and another belonging to The Human League, one of Sheffield's most enduring bands from the 1980s.

The Showroom shows up to 500 films a year, as many as most multiplexes, and its programming is a discerning mixture of the best of the new releases with a quirky diet of unusual international films. Fancy seeing the latest films by a wonderful director from Senegal? Caught up on what South Korea has been making recently? This is the place for you. It is best known internationally for hosting the annual Doc/Fest in June, which draws in nosy parkers from Hollywood. Louis Theroux makes an annual pilgrimage every year. Martin Scorsese has done a Skype interview.

Address 15 Paternoster Row, S1 2BX, +44 (0)114 275 7727, www.showroomworkstation.org.uk | Getting there Less than 5-minute walk from Sheffield Station and Interchange, following signs to the city centre, where the Showroom is diagonally across from The Howard pub | Hours Consult website for screening times | Tip Fusion Cafe at 74 Arundel Street has its own bakery and crafts gallery and is a few minutes away on foot (www.academyofmakers.co.uk/fusion-cafe.html).

86 Skye Edge
The pigeon fanciers' paradise

The alarmingly steep, headlong-down-plunging length of Sheffield hillside beautifully named Skye Edge is a cold, hard-bitten, narrow tract of high, scrubby ground with tussocky grass in abundance much beloved by the pigeon fanciers of Sheffield.

From here you can get a nearly perfect overview of the city centre – it's a breathtaking panoramic sweep – and of Bramall Lane too, Sheffield United's ground since 1889, together with the magnificent green dome of the Al Masjid Mosque on Wolseley Road.

It is here that quad-bikers race their machines, people dump their unloved mattresses, old prams, ancient rain-sodden carpets and the odd smashed umbrella, and where the pigeon fanciers keep their favourite birds in a cluster of wooden pigeon lofts cum shacks, which seem to march, rather precariously, step by step, down the hillside, made safe from thieves by powerful lengths of corrugated iron. Many squeezed dry Stella artois cans are to be found amongst the brambles.

Where the Edge levels out along the top, there's a soccer pitch for whoever happens along. The pigeons here - there are about 200 of them in all - are racing birds, and they are put through their paces from this Edge from April to September, often on three-day races that will take them several hundred miles from their homes on this Sheffield hillside. The shortest race is 100 miles. The fanciers themselves are a dedicated bunch, often going back several generations.

It is here that the birds are looked after: fed, trained, cleaned and bred. The queen pigeon is treated with especial care: she has her own loft. There's money in it too, from betting relatively modest sums. It also costs to send the birds off racing. The young stay with their parents until they're twenty-five days old. The names of the local places are haunted by the presence of birds too: Kestrel Green, Wren Bank, Quail Rise…

Address Close to Skye Edge Avenue, S2 5DP | Getting there Bus 120 from Park Hill | Hours Unrestricted | Tip Try Lotte on the Edge at 14 Union Road for a good coffee.

87__Stanage Edge

The climbers grip on for dear life

Sheffield is a city where the Great Outdoors is forever knocking on the door, beckoning you out yonder to sniff the higher, purer air. It is at its most challengingly dramatic out west at Stanage Edge, that point where Yorkshire and Derbyshire abut, where rough millstone grit country – snatch up a fragment and you feel immediately its crumbly grittiness – runs up against limestone. This is where the climbers and the boulderers come flocking, from the world over, to tackle one or another of its hundreds of climbing challenges, each one of which is precisely documented.

The sweep of the edge as you approach from a distance, the majesty of all this megalithic scenery, is quite breathtaking: a semicircular escarpment of over three miles of great, overhanging buttresses of compacted grey rocks, each one bearing down upon another. There are views from its top of the sweep of the Hope Valley and the surrounding peaks and villages: Mam Tor, Kinderscout, Castleton... Most interesting of all is to approach the edge, by foot, from below, pushing your way up along some foot-worn, fern-brushed, pack-horse trail with its lichen and its harebells, until you are standing amongst the climbers themselves at the alarmingly exhilarating base of the overhanging edge itself, and then stare up at the jutting flanks of rock, some fat, broad and boastful, others thinnish wedges which look as if they might just have inveigled themselves into the gang. Some outcrops look almost human – sculpted. Is that a lip or a chin? You watch the climbers huddling together, cracking a joke or two, as they leaf through their guide book to *Eastern Grit*, and then set their colourful ropes, metal tackle and chalk in order. (You need chalk on palm and finger ends to help you grip on for dear life.) Every climb has its own name, and is ranked in order of difficulty. Is it to be Cemetery Waits today, pal?

Address Stanage Edge, grid reference SK 245829 | Getting there No direct public transport: bus 51 from High Street to Lodge Moor terminus, then approximately 3 miles' walk along Redmires Road, and then by-way; train to Hathersage, and walk from there only suitable for hikers; or car: from A 57 at Crosspool take Sandygate Road, then continue along Redmires Road, on-street parking on Redmires Road | Hours Unrestricted | Tip Visit the Weston Park Museum if you want to become better acquainted with the dramatic geology of the Sheffield region.

88__Stanage Pole

An ancient waymarker in the wilderness

Landscapes always demand vantage points, and Sheffield, being deep-mined by river valleys, has more than most. One of its finest, loneliest, bleakest (in the winter months), and most comprehensively sweeping, is at a most mysterious place called Stanage Pole, where a tall, dark finger of wood fashioned from a single larch tree, hemmed in by slabs of millstone grit (just comfortable enough for picnickers to regard as seats on a clement afternoon), rises up, slightly waveringly, slightly self-doubtingly – and certainly not imperiously. It looks and feels a little fragile, up here on these wind-bitten moorland heights. To reach it, you walk steadily uphill on a track beyond the third of the Redmires dams, flanking a plantation of conifers on your right, climbing steadily between heather and ling, glimpsing flighty wisps of bog cotton that you are too wise to cull.

What is a lonely pole doing here, so close to Stanage Edge? Yes, from here 10 minutes' walk will take you to the very edge of that climber's natural wonder-wall, where you can see hardy rock-grapplers, surrounded by coils of colourful rope and gleaming metal tackle, dangling their legs into the abyss. And an odd faithful dog.

A metal disc at the pole's base tells you what you will identify if you look towards all points of the compass – directly west, for example, is Hathersage, where the ancient packhorse trail you have probably been walking along to reach this far, marked at ground level by scooped-out slabs of millstone grit, would have taken you in the end. This old mute pole speaks of far more than curiosity points on a compass. It tells of the limits of ancient kingdoms – this is where Mercia may have ended and Northumbria began. It speaks of the limits of ecclesiastical jurisdiction too – Canterbury ceded her authority to York here. It is also where Yorkshire ends and Derbyshire begins.

Address Hallam Moors, grid reference SK 2468784429 | Getting there No direct public transport: bus 51 from High Street to Lodge Moor terminus then 3-mile walk along Redmires Road, and then by-way; train to Hathersage, but walk from there only suitable for hikers; or car: take A 57 to Crosspool, then Sandygate Road, then continue along Redmires Road, on-street parking on Redmires Road beside Redmires Reservoir | Hours Unrestricted | Tip Travelling by car back past the third and last of the Redmires Dams, look out for a small sign to your left which will lead you to Hammond's Field Nature Reserve, where, if your luck is in, you may see a lapwing or a curlew.

89 — Stanley Cook's House

A poet's window on a strangely familiar world

This solid, dependable house in north-east Sheffield, with its twisty steps up to the front door, set well back from the road and at a high vantage point, situated at a moment when the hill seems to pause and almost begin to level off before beginning its long climb again in the general direction of Barnsley, was once occupied by Stanley Cook, Sheffield's greatest post-war poet. It has been for sale, repeatedly, in recent years. Does the very fabric of the house slightly regret his absence?

Stanley Cook raised a family of two girls and a boy here, and was a teacher of English at the local grammar school a 15-minute walk further up the hill; he did that walk most days. He died in 1991. His study, where he wrote his poetry at his desk in long-hand, was at the front of the house (it's the window on the left, on the ground floor), and behind that desk hung a painting by a local artist called R. W. Pugsley, painted in 1975, of a globe, two flowerpots and an astronomical instrument, set in front of a window. It was a clear-eyed, unpretentious piece of work, hiding nothing, and it seemed to say: this is how it is. Its title was *The World in the Classroom Window*.

Stanley Cook's poetry was like that. His preoccupation as a poet was with the locals who passed by in the road outside a window such as this one – how people around these parts lived, behaved, carried themselves, eked out their proud and meagre lives, clinging on to respectability for dear life; thumbnail sketches of the sobering reality of day-to-day make-do. A bookish man, of few words when spoken to, and those words always well chosen, well crafted, he looked hard and steadily at the world. And steady was his walk too, when he ascended the hill to Firth Park Grammar School in his long, dark winter coat, just a little stooped over in thought, carrying a saggy leather bag full of school exercise books.

Address 600 Barnsley Road, S5 6UA | Getting there Bus 1, 1a or 88 from Arundel Gate to Barnsley Road (Northern General Hospital); or car: take A 6135 (towards Chapeltown) from city centre to Barnsley Road, on-street parking | Hours Unrestricted | Tip If you walk down Barnsley Road towards Fir Vale, St Cuthbert's church will be on your left just as you reach the traffic lights. It has a wonderful east window by Archibald Davies of the Bromsgrove Guild, a disciple of William Morris.

90 St Marie's Cathedral

Pugin's exquisite gift to Sheffield

When London's Houses of Parliament were rebuilt after the devastating fire of 1834, Augustus Pugin, designer, and architect of the Gothic Revival, played a major role in their reconstruction. He also took a keen interest in the creation of St Marie's, Sheffield's Roman Catholic cathedral, advising his friend, the cathedral's principal architect, Matthew Hadfield, on such questions as the height of the screen behind the high altar. Some of Pugin's work has been destroyed: the high altar itself, for example, which was replaced in the 1920s, though the new may also contain elements of the old. Are these lovely angels at either end of that altar screen by him? They may be. A building such as this one, full of the accretions of history, distant and recent, can be such a guessing game. He also designed the west window, and the cathedral's magnificent chalice, kept for safety in a stout black cube of an old battered wooden box, which can be seen only on Sheffield's annual Heritage Days. What a gleaming surprise it is though!

The cathedral's finest treasures, seven alabaster panels showing scenes from Christ's life and the Passion – dramatic sculptural scenes recessed into small, rectangular frames – are not by Pugin at all. Several may, at least in part, be medieval. Why such doubt? They were found near Exeter Cathedral in 1845, and may have been reconstructed by a local antiques dealer. There are some odd combinations of body parts if you look closely. Their restoration is often crude too – poorly modelled heads on top of ancient torsos. They were gifted to St Marie's around 1847, and displayed in the mortuary chapel. In the 1970s, when the cathedral was renovated, they were put into storage by ham-fisted handlers, who damaged them again. In 2015 they were finally restored. Look carefully at them. There is the drama of El Greco in at least one of them.

Address Cathedral House, Norfolk Street, S1 2JB, +44 (0)114 272 2522, www.stmariecathedral.org, office@stmariecathedral.org | Getting there 1-minute walk from Sheffield City Hall, taking first right off the top end of Fargate | Hours Mon–Fri 7.30am–6pm, Sat 7.30am–5pm, Sun 7.30am–7.30pm | Tip An excellent Italian restaurant, VeroGusto, is almost directly opposite the cathedral entrance.

91 St Paul's, Parson Cross

By the architect of Coventry Cathedral

Marooned beside a road in north-west Sheffield, set amidst a post-war housing estate whose roads were built by German and Italian prisoners of war, is a church which seems to have no name, because it has no notice board. This church, built in 1959, was dedicated to St Paul. Its architect was a man called Basil Spence who, three years later, would create a new cathedral at Coventry on the site of a bombed-out shell.

The church feels starkly modern and ancient – simultaneously. Its ancient feel can be attributed to the fact that, like so many medieval churches in Italy, its tower stands quite separate from the main body of the church. In other respects, the gaunt, functional simplicity of this tower of brick and concrete could not be more representative of its era. Two tall brick walls are separated from each other by vertical concrete ties. Between those ties, close to the top, a cross hangs suspended. You seem to see through it, as if there is nothing to hide. You approach the entrance to the church by walking beneath a covered canopy of tubular steel and concrete.

Inside, this sense of honest-to-god openness, this belief that there is to be nothing illusory about a building, continues. The church is a single broad, light-flooded room. No aisles. Instead of a colourful east window behind the high altar that prevents the eye seeing through to the world beyond, there are generous panels of plain glass to stare through as you sit in your pew. To the left and the right of a latticed wooden screen, you can watch a mother pushing her baby or read a sign announcing Sid's Fish Bar. The side walls of the church are of stark, bare red brick. Their angled sections give them rhythm, a movement backwards and forwards. The roof is gently bowed. This church is a magnificent tribute to the power of modest means.

Address Wordsworth Avenue, S5, +44 (0)114 296 2320, mail@jdroch.com | **Getting there** Bus 7 or 8 from Arundel Gate stops almost outside the Church; or car: take A 61 north, and turn off on the B 6087, on-street parking | **Hours** Sun 10.30am – noon | **Tip** A magnificent ancient church is nearby: Ecclesfield Parish Church.

92__ The Steelworker

Hard-bitten, with tight muffler at neck

Art can sometimes take the form of a *memento mori*, a reminder of how a life – and the toil that can consume so much of that life – was once lived. The axe that was taken to so much of the steel industry during the Thatcher years during the 1980s was commemorated during that same decade by Sheffield City Council, which commissioned painter Paul Waplington from Nottingham, who also did a fine painting of one of the oldest buildings of Sheffield University, to create a portrait of a typical steelworker in 1986. The result is *The Steelworker*, a mural in brick, a bit like a mosaic of the kind at which the Romans were once so adept, complete with a white muffler around his throat. He has eyes of an almost unearthly size – blame or praise the size of the bricks used for this fascinating little quirk.

The huge portrait almost emerges from the gable end of the building that contains it and shows it off. He is a proud grafter, hard-bitten by years of hot, dangerous, relentless, and physically demanding work, with his cleft chin, jug ears, and hard bitten gaze that seems to suggest indomitability, coupled with a bit of jaunty good cheer into the bargain. His expression looks as if he is trying to make an even bigger splash out in the world beyond the constraints of the four-story building that frames his face.

The muffler tight at his throat is particularly fascinating to contemplate. So characteristic of its time, a mix of grey edging off to white in this portrait – why would a steelworker, who endured a working life forever on the sweat, wear a white muffler of all things? Nothing better than white for showing off muck and grime and sweat. And that's what was always so noticeable when a steelworker got off the bus from down Savile Street to wend his weary way back home: his face rigid and seamed with exhaustion, and his muffler looking scruffy around his neck.

Address 11 Castle Street, Sheffield S3 8LT | Getting there 5 minutes' wallk from any bus stop in city centre | Hours Unrestricted | Tip Visit Fagan's at 69 Broad Lane, a ten-minute walk from here, one of Sheffield's most iconic pubs, part owned by the drummer of the Arctic Monkeys.

93 Strip the Willow

Everything comes in for something

Two hefty fellas are lifting a front door out, and stacking it against the neighbour's wall. Not for long though. It will be shoved into the back of a van before you can blink. Ay, it's all go at Strip the Willow. The entranceway is spilling over with precariously stacked furniture, planks piled ten or so high, up-ended stools, a teetering wardrobe or two, leaning mantelpieces. An entire crate is brimming with table legs of assorted vintage. There's old furniture here, and lots of new furniture made from old, with recycled wood. Everything comes in for something. Nothing's wasted. Well, it's not so much recycling as upcycling: the new pieces made from all these old bits and pieces look very handsome, it has to be said. Fancy a garden bench for £65?

You weave your way through a cobbled yard to the workshop at the back where Alex, the 25-year-old apprentice joiner from the Gleadless Valley – he's been learning and practising his trade here for three years – is standing near his lathe, dusting the sawdust off his hands. There's a Welsh dresser in the making just nearby, clamped fast in several vises so that it will keep its shape as the glue sets. Walls are hung with saws, the ceiling with ladders – it's a bit like a conjuring trick. The transparent boxes on the stacked shelving are full of drawer handles, washers, screws. Everything's in the making and the remaking.

For Jon Johnson, the man who spent 26 years with South Yorkshire Police before creating this business in 2013 (he took early retirement at the age of 47), it's all about community enterprise, giving jobs to those who need them, nurturing skills, bringing people together. He dreamt up the idea after walking back from the Broadfield, a local pub, with a couple of pints inside him.

His latest venture is the boldest of all: to convert shipping containers into affordable homes.

Address 226b Sharrow View Road, S7 1DF, +44 (0)7948 033859, www.stripthewillow.org | **Getting there** Bus 4 or 4a from Sheffield Interchange to top of Cemetery Road, then walk down Sharrow Lane to first right, Sharrow View Road; on-street parking | **Hours** Mon–Sat 10am–4pm | **Tip** Get a lovely Turkish wet shave, with a warm cosseting towel, from Marmaris Barbers nearby.

94 Tamper: Sellers Wheel

A Kiwi coffee shop wings in from the Pacific

There's a sizeable community of Kiwis of the human persuasion in Sheffield, and they often tend to congregate at a relaxing coffee-bar-cum-eaterie called Tamper: Sellers Wheel. The business was established seven years ago by one of their own, a man called Jon Perry from Wellington who married a local girl from Rotherham, and took root here. (Friday nights are especially good because the place stays open until 10pm for food, wine, beer and cocktails.)

Jon's ambition was to create a Sheffield version of a Kiwi coffee shop, with products and vibe to match (did you know that flat white was a Kiwi invention?), and so he established it in an old silversmith's factory, which is why a succession of fine brick arches defines the shape of the long eating-area's ceiling. This room, with its procession of steel columns, and its pleasingly weathered central table, still feels haunted by the ghosts of craftsmen of yore on the factory floor. At the back of the room, where a wall has been cut through to enable you to spy on chefs at work, a mural by Faunagraphic, a prolific Sheffield street artist, shows a Kiwi (of the bird variety) boldly striding through vegetation as vibrantly colourful and naively luxurious as something that might have been painted by Henri Rousseau in the Paris of a century and a half ago. Everything is home made and locally sourced, and the Kiwi dishes on offer (the place had a Samoan chef until quite recently) include a classic mince on toasted ciabatta (the mince is a pleasingly robust amalgam of pulled beef and pork), with free range egg and hollandaise sauce. Given that the place is locally rooted too, the condiments dish offers Sheffield's very own Henderson's Relish. Treat yourself to a lamington as you pay at the till – vanilla sponge with chocolate ganache and grated coconut, just in case you're asking. Come early for lunch because they don't take bookings.

Address 149 Arundel Street, S1 2NU, +44 (0)114 275 7970, www.tampercoffee.co.uk |
Getting there 5-minute walk from Sheffield Station up Howard Street then left into
Arundel Street | Hours Mon–Sat 8am–4.30pm, Sun 9am–4.30pm | Tip Almost opposite
the front door you'll see a courtyard across the street. Go and admire the great brick chimney
of the Butcher Works of 1835, amidst buildings often used for Victorian film settings.

95_ The Thryft House Yew Tree
Older than Magna Carta

Sheffield's oldest living thing is rooted in the garden of a farmhouse near Ringinglow. It is an ancient yew tree which may once have served as a boundary marker between parishes – or perhaps even between the ancient kingdoms of Northumbria and Mercia. Its estimated longevity – at least 800 years, but possibly a good deal more – quite takes the breath away. Its girth is elephantine: a standard tape measure fails to encompass it by about a metre, which means that its corpulence – it seems to crave a bit of humanising chat – is in excess of six metres. Could this tree have been alive when humans were whispering about, say, the accession of Henry II, first of the Plantagenets in 1154? Well, er, yes.

Its appearance is as extraordinary as its longevity. It seems to exist somewhere between life and death. The centre looks hollowed out, like a dark sea grotto. One of its sides seems to have died long ago, and yet its living foliage on the opposing side of the tree suggests otherwise: that it is not only clinging onto its preciously fragile life, but that it somehow also possesses the power to regenerate itself, perhaps magically. Like those hardy thistles once written about by the Yorkshire poet Ted Hughes in a poem of that name, it is accepting of death, but only to a degree. It is also fighting back over the same ground. All told, there is an aura of magic about its entire appearance. It looks as if it is more bone than wood. In fact, it is more a monumental sculptural object, Sheffield's finest without a doubt, than a mere tree. It fingers skyward, twistily, nervily, with a shocking degree of self-dramatisation. Its colours – grey, blue, green or coppery – seem to be an amalgam of many colours, all subtly blended, depending upon the angle at which the light hits it. We feel humbled to be in the presence of such ancientness.

A tree can feel like a miracle in a well tended garden.

Address Ringinglow Road, S11 7TA | Getting there 10-minute walk along Ringinglow Road to just past Silverdale School on left; bus 83 or 88 from Leopold Street to Bents Green; or car: from A 625 take Ringinglow Road | Hours Private garden, viewings strictly by appointment only, contact dgwestaway@yahoo.co.uk | Tip Lovers of extraordinary trees need to visit the recently restored Victorian glasshouses of Sheffield's Botanical Gardens.

96_ Tinsley Canal Walk

Nature's quietly determined fightback

Canal walks through places where industry once flourished can offer unexpected natural bounties. The serene set-apartness of the Tinsley Canal, threading its way along the Don Valley in the general direction of Rotherham, is no exception. Ten minutes along a tow path whose edges are dressed with stone – once a place fit only for toiling horses – that leads you out of Victoria Quays in Sheffield city centre, you come across swags of blackberries ripe for the picking, tucked in beside a red-brick wall. Moored to the further bank, a houseboat called Rocinante, its handsome, brass-rimmed portholes buffed up to a high gleam, is wallowing low and secretive in the water. There used to be a lot of light industry abutting this waterway. Some of it clings on still, skeletally beautiful now in its gentle dereliction. The red window frames of Roofing Solutions are reflected in the water like ghostly, shifting calligraphy. Every so often a bridge flings its shapely back across the water. Each one is named and numbered. The arch of the bridge at Bacon Lane, built in 1819, looks bitten into, like cheese. As you pass beneath it, you can see how the horses' ropes have sawed into the soft stone.

Along the entire length of this once dirty waterside, nature is fighting back: water lilies float on the water; silver birches show off their spindly shapeliness; buddleia and dog roses vie for attention.

The fishermen you meet from time to time can describe the varieties of fish they haul in from these once filthy waters and – usually – put back (gently, one points out): tench, roach, perch, bream. Or even a carp, up to 24 lbs in weight. The greatest surprise is waiting as you approach the Tinsley Viaduct: an entire colony of wild fig trees on the farther bank, the largest such colony in the United Kingdom. The warm, once polluted waters caused them to flourish here.

They look as happy as Larry.

Address Victoria Quays, S2 | Getting there 10-minute walk from Sheffield Station via Park Square roundabout and fifth exit signposted Victoria Quays; on-site parking at Victoria Quays | Hours Unrestricted | Tip Look out for the curved terrace of coal merchants' offices (c. 1870) as you begin your walk from Victoria Quays.

97___Two Steps to Heaven

The gentle art of eating fish and chips

There's nothing quite like fish and chips bought from a local Sheffield chippy, lightly salted, and with a sprinkling of malt vinegar. As the poet Stanley Cook, chronicler of Sheffield life, once expressed it in a poem: 'Out of the paper bag, / comes the hot breath of the chips, / And I shall blow on them / to stop them burning my lips…'

Two Steps is not only one of the longest lived – it first opened in 1895 – but it's also one of the best. For the last 15 years it's been run by Laggy Kafetzis, who was born above a coffee shop called Galaxy in Birmingham. His grandfather came to England from Larnaca in Cyprus in the 1950s, and opened a hotel in Weston-super-Mare. Why *Two Steps* though? During World War II there were five chippies in the area. This was the only one with two steps up… You can read about its history on the walls.

A chippy is not a sitting down sort of place. It's generally quite small and table-less, and with a high counter, in front of which the queue forms, and behind which you can watch all the action: chips being crozzled – a good Sheffield word that, snatched from steel-making – to perfection in a gleaming metal trough of spitting fat. And then, close by, there's another trough for the fillets of cod or haddock, which come out with a brown toasting of crispy batter. The fryer darts from one to the other, heaving out the chips in mesh baskets, then plunging in more to the accompaniment of a dangerous roar of sizzling fat. Everything is lined up for inspection in the hot cabinet you lean against as you patiently queue: cod, haddock, fish rissoles, sausages, Yorkshire fish cakes. Oh, and don't forget the side dish of mushy peas in batter, and perhaps even a pickled onion from the big glass jar.

Fish and chips come wrapped in paper, open. Don't forget to pick up one of those little two-pronged wooden forks to scoff them with.

Address 249 Sharrow Vale Road, S11 8ZE, +44 (0)114 266 5694 | Getting there Bus 81, 82, 83, 83a or 88 from Leopold Street to Ecclesall Road and walk down Hickmott Road; or 10 minutes by car from city centre, just off A 625, on-street parking nearby | Hours Mon–Sat 11.30am–2pm, 5–9pm | Tip The Beer House, a lovely micro-pub, is at 623 Ecclesall Road, just five minutes' walk away. Six hand-pulled local ales are usually on offer.

98__ Turner Museum of Glass

Cinderella locked in a Sheffield cabinet

If you were looking for Cinderella in Sheffield, where exactly might you expect to find her? Inside the Turner Museum of Glass at the University of Sheffield there is a tall, locked, glazed cabinet, recessed into a wall, where you can see a headless mannequin wearing a blue, ankle-length wedding dress. Just beside her, displayed on clear glass shelves as if afloat on air, there is a small clasp bag and matching blue hat, ranged one above the other. The mannequin seems to be leaning slightly towards us, as if confiding something. All these objects belonged to a Scotswoman called Helen Nairn Monro, who became the second wife of W. E. S. Turner, the founder of this museum, on 1 July, 1943. She herself was a glass artist, and her wish as a new wife was to be married in a glass dress. And this is precisely what we are staring at: a dress, slippers, hat and bag, all fashioned from spun glass. And all rather uncomfortable, remarks John Parker, the curator of the museum, who is standing nearby. The slippers especially, heavy and uncomfortable, which made her foot bleed.

The rest of this museum, which largely consists of Turner's own collection of glass amassed over a period of 30 years, comprises both a brief history of glassmaking from ancient Egypt onwards – the earliest objects are from the reign of Rameses IV – and many unique samples of 20th-century studio glass from the various countries that Turner visited. He himself became professor of the world's very first Department of Glass Technology, and he saw it as his role to be a mediator between science and industry – there was much glassmaking going on in the environs of Sheffield, but the industry was notoriously secretive about its methods of making. Turner opened it up a little, and his many friends and contacts often gave him unique, experimental pieces, many of which can be seen here today.

It's a world tour of 20th century studio glass in miniature.

Address Department of Materials Science & Engineering, Portobello Street, S1 4DT, www.turnermuseum.group.shef.ac.uk, j.m.parker@sheffield.ac.uk | **Getting there** Bus 95 from Sheffield Interchange to West Street; tram to West Street, opposite Mappin Street; or car: Q Park, Rockingham Street car park | **Hours** Mon–Fri 10am–4pm | **Tip** Look out for the roaring, gilded tiger on the façade of Tiger Works in West Street, a sculptural trademark above one of Sheffield's most popular bars.

99__Upper Chapel Forecourt

Quietly reflecting upon popular dissent

There is no audience more difficult to please than a Sheffield audience, the Yorkshire actor and stand-up comic Big Mick Walters once said. Why? Could this be to do with the fact that cutlery was Sheffield's most important industry for centuries, and that cutlers, by and large, those men who work for themselves in small, pent spaces, learnt a proud, cussed, nay-saying spirit of independence that seems to be in the marrow of every Sheffielder's bones?

There is no quieter spot to reflect upon the history of popular dissent in Sheffield, whether it be religious or political, than on one of the benches of the lovely, set-apart forecourt of the Upper Chapel in Norfolk Street. Its neoclassical façade once faced in the opposite direction altogether, towards the common hubbub of Fargate. You will find yourself sharing the space with sculptures of local folk by George Fullard, people without pretension who feel just right here. One is an angry woman whose dress seems to have been buffeted naughtily by the wind. Another is a mother dandling her baby on her knee. A third one runs.

James Fisher established its first congregation, in 1662. After the restoration of the monarchy, he refused to swear allegiance to England's established church, and he was duly evicted from his job at the parish church, which later became Sheffield's cathedral. He established a community of dissenters along with a group of like-minded friends. He was preyed upon by his enemies for his disobedience, and sent to jail, where he was deprived of his rights. His friends could not see him. All writing materials were forbidden. Sick and enfeebled, he died soon after his release.

As you rise to leave, look at the gravestones across which you are walking. The words on them are so simple, and the memorials to the dead so plain and unadorned. That says something about Sheffield.

Address Norfolk Street, S1 2JD, +44 (0)114 272 8174, www.upperchapelsheffield.org.uk | **Getting there** City-centre buses to Norfolk Street; tram to Cathedral; or Q Park Charles Street car park or pay-and-display parking on Norfolk Street | **Hours** Unrestricted | **Tip** George Fullard's sketchbooks and drawings can be seen in the archive of Sheffield School of Art (www.libguides.shu.ac.uk/specialcollection/georgefullard).

100_ Upper Wincobank Chapel

A modest slice of New England piety

Wincobank Undenominational Chapel, which nestles in the lee of Wincobank Hill in north Sheffield, feels a little like a tiny slice of modest New England piety miraculously transported to England. Its interior, with its original wooden pews and pipe organ, has a lovely sobriety. At the back is propped a huge Sunday-school banner, once paraded at Whitsuntide.

The chapel was built in 1841 in the garden of Wincobank Hall, which was the home of two remarkable sisters, Mary Anne Rawson and Emily Read. Two plaques inside the chapel commemorate them. Beneath Emily's plaque, there is a reproduction of a painting held at the National Portrait Gallery in London. It is a crowded group portrait by Benjamin Robert Haydon (painter of grandiose historical scenes) of all those present at the Anti-Slavery Convention in London in 1840. Most are men, of course, but on the extreme right there is a small huddle of women, and the one most vividly present to us, thanks to her lustrously pearly complexion and her frilly bonnet, is Mary Anne Rawson of Sheffield, one of the city's great political agitators. The sisters helped to make this chapel possible, and it was created, in part, to provide free education for the children of the poor. The building served two purposes at once. It was both a day school and a place of worship. Its priority, above all things else, was the education of children. Emily did much of the teaching at the chapel. Mary Anne was involved in the attempt to abolish slavery in the colonies. She would travel the streets of Sheffield trying to persuade women to stop buying their sugar. When Mary Anne Rawson grew too weak to walk to her chapel at the bottom of the garden, she would be carried there in her own sedan chair.

Address Wincobank Avenue, S5 6BB, +44 (0)79801 43776, www.wincobankchapel.org, uwuchapel@gmail.com | Getting there Bus 95 or 95a from city centre or Meadowhall Interchange to Wincobank Avenue; or car: take B 6082, via Newman Road and Wincobank Avenue, on-street parking | Hours Tue 10am – noon, service Sun 11am – noon | Tip On the little green across the road from the chapel, you can enjoy sitting in one or another of a little huddle of Enchanted Chairs.

101__ Vulcan

Sheffield's forge-master general

The god Vulcan, that hammer-wielding patron of smiths and crafts-men, is an apt symbol for a city celebrated down the centuries for the forging of metal. He is on the city's coat of arms – and in the open air, too. This sculpture, cast in bronze, stands, naked to the wind, on the very pinnacle of the Town Hall at the city's centre, teetering on one leg, and gesturing balletically in the general direction of flocks of wheeling pigeons. An Italian sculptor called Mario Raggi made him, in 1897, and a brave steeplejack, Cromwell W. Hartley, posi-tioned him there. (Mario Raggi had his triumphs elsewhere too. In 1883, his statue of Prime Minister Benjamin Disraeli was unveiled in London's Parliament Square, where it still stands.)

In the third decade of the 20th century, Sheffielders were so proud to have Vulcan watching over them that a telescope was installed in Barker's Pool (but is sadly no longer there) to enable the eager voyeur to get a much closer look at him for a penny a go. The passage of time has lent him an oddly greenish hue.

Those with knowledge of Greek or Roman mythology might have been surprised to note quite how much the modern Vulcan presid-ing over the fortunes of Sheffield industry differed from the god of classical antiquity. The pagan original, he who set up his forge on Mount Olympus for the making of arrows, sickles, thunderbolts and other things of potentially deadly use, was often said to be stocky, corpulent, clumsy of gait, with a bad limp. This Vulcan, in his slen-der, muscular agility, has been thoroughly Italianised. He inhabits a world which has long since profited by the sculptural triumphs of Michelangelo. The many retellings of Vulcan's story remind us that he was not merely a forge-master, adept at the making and repairing of weaponry, but was also called upon to cook the wedding breakfast for Cupid and Psyche.

Address Surrey Street, S1 2HH | Getting there 10-minute walk from bus and train stations; buses passing through city centre will stop nearby; tram to Cathedral; or car: Q Park Charles Street car park | Hours Unrestricted | Tip Vulcan will have been intrigued to spot the arrival of *Women of Steel* in 2016, at the top end of Barker's Pool, a sculptural tribute to all those local women who served in the steel industry during two world wars.

102 — Walking Man
How a gait can define a character

The folk of Sheffield have a very particular way of walking. It combines doggedness with a certain resignation; a straight-into-the-wind purposefulness with an acute awareness of bodily fragility, and an acknowledgement that there may be resistance to be encountered along the way.

Sheffield is one of those places that demand footfalls above all things else. To pass through by automated means, at high speed, never does justice to the glories of the countryside that this city, in part, encompasses, or to the wondrous extent of its ancient woodlands and its encircling parklands. There are more trees here per head of population than there are in any other European city. This is a city where the countryside is nudging to get in.

George Fullard, the sculptor of this piece, was a man hobbled by the tragedy of war. Severely wounded at the Battle of Monte Cassino in 1944, he died far too young. His *Walking Man* seems to be a Sheffielder through and through: independent-spirited, determined to get to where he has decided to go. It stands on its own little stretch of raised pavement, facing two theatres – the Victorian Lyceum and the Crucible, famous for its thrust stage, which enables the audience to experience the action from all three sides, and, of course, for playing host to the World Snooker Championship, so adored by the Chinese.

Walking Man, one of life's eternal pedestrians, is ready for inclement weather – his collar is turned up. He is thin as a blade, too – there seems to be precious little to him beneath the voluminous flow of the overcoat. He is a working man through and through. George's father was famous as a local socialist playwright, and his childhood, lived in a small house in working-class Darnall, was full of trade union banter. This is a picture, in bronze, of stoicism and resolve rolled into one. The walking will never end.

Address Surrey Street, outside the entrance to the Winter Garden in Tudor Square | Getting there 10-minute walk from bus and train stations; buses passing through city centre stop nearby; tram to Cathedral; or car: Q Park Charles Street car park | Hours Unrestricted | Tip Almost directly across from the sculpture is a plaque in memory of Thomas Boulsover, the inventor of Old Sheffield Plate.

103_ The Wantley Dragon
The mythical creature with fourteen eyes

The legend of the terrible dragon of Wantley, that great devourer of children, and how he was vanquished by the brave knight of More Hall in his fearsome spiked armour (hand-forged in Sheffield perhaps), still swirls in the air above the Don Valley just north of Sheffield. This dragon, with his seven heads, fourteen eyes, and four creaking wings, had a nose which ran with smouldering snot. Apparently. The dragon's cave was said to be set somewhere high up on Wharncliffe Crags, from where, looking up-valley, you can nowadays catch a glimpse of the Tata steelworks of Stocksbridge, and, just below and to your right as you look down from the crags' steepling immensity, the bypass which zips you off in the general direction of Manchester.

The story of this dragon has been made and remade on umpteen occasions – like any good suit of armour. A ballad telling of his extravagant exploits was included in a collection called *Percy's Reliques* in the 18th century. An opera about the dragon-vanquishing knight took Covent Garden by storm in the 1730s. That one, though still cloaked in misty medieval trappings, was political satire aimed at the pernicious taxation policies of the government of Robert Walpole. The dragon then re-emerged some years later at the opening of Sir Walter Scott's *Ivanhoe*.

To see the dragon's head now, realised as a sculpture in elm by Mark Bell, and cunningly extended at its lashing tail-end by a serpentining length of drystone wall courtesy of John Alston, you have to climb uphill into Bitholmes Wood. He lies there in a clearing, jaws agape, waiting to breathe hellfire and brimstone onto you. The original More Hall still exists, though it is well hidden away these days behind a modest screen of trees near to the Bolsterstone Reservoir. Mercifully, it is now owned by the peaceable editor of a Catholic weekly newspaper.

Address Bitholmes Wood, More Hall Lane, Oughtibridge, S36 | Getting there Bus 57 from Sheffield Interchange to Manchester Road / More Hall Lane, then walk up More Hall Lane toward Bolsterstone to a sign on right marking the entrance to Bitholmes Wood – this track will lead you to the dragon; or car: take A 61 (North) then A 6102 | Hours Unrestricted | Tip The Blue Ball at Wharncliffe Side, the closest village, features a succulent steak night on Mondays and Fridays between 5 and 9pm. Good local ales too.

104__ Weston Park Weather Station

Utterly dependable, rain, sleet or shine

Hi-tech? You must be joking. The utterly dependable, utterly unassuming Weston Park Weather Station, one of the oldest in the country, is a remarkably uncomplicated affair. The little that there is of it sits on a small rectangle of ground behind a high fence at the top end of one of Sheffield's most shapely small parks, which abuts the original red-brick buildings of Sheffield University. It has been giving remarkably accurate predictions, daily, since 1882.

It consists of two rain measures. One is a bucket that tips when filled with water, and the other a funnel. There are also some soil thermometers at different depths – 30 cm and 100 cm deep. Other thermometers are kept inside the Stevenson Screen, which looks a little like a white box with slatted walls, raised up on thin, tall, metal, trestle-table legs. It could easily be a companionable rabbit hutch. Inside the Stevenson Screen there are other thermometers, for checking maximum and minimum temperatures. The slatted walls give protection from solar radiation or ferocious gusts of wind. There is also a patch of bare soil at the far end for checking the condition of the ground. Is it frozen today or dry? Workers at Weston Park Museum – just yards away – collect the data, and use it to answer thousands of enquiries every year. They also send it on to the Met Office. One of the museum's first curators, Elijah Howarth, set the station up. He had such a passion for recording the happy vicissitudes of Sheffield's weather that he was popularly known as Elijah the Prophet. Such information could be of great practical use to the local mining industry. Changes in air pressure had an impact upon the safety of workers underground. Elijah kept up his good work for 47 years, and he was never happier than when the weather was being eccentric.

No unauthorised entry

In the event of an emergency contact the
Met Office Weather Desk on 0870 900 0100

Address Weston Park, S10 | Getting there Bus 52 from Church Street to Sheffield
Children's Hospital, you'll find the weather station in front of Weston Park Museum; or car:
take A 57 out of the city centre (direction Glossop), on-street parking | Hours Unrestricted |
Tip If you walk to the delightful Japanese Bridge (designed by Robert Marnock) at the
bottom of the park, you will then have the option to feed the waterfowl.

105__ The Wicker Arches

The honey glow of stone from Wharncliffe Crags

It is the yawning reach of the central span, its breadth, its depth, its elegance, which enthrals the eye. The stone glows like honey in the sun. The whole structure has a kind of rude, solid magnificence, from the hefty keystones of the side arches, which look as if they might have been driven in by a mallet, to the long, overhanging entablature, and the way the blocks of stone spread sideways across the central arch, in a graceful sweeping motion. A low-relief sculpture set into a rectangular niche in one of the side arches shows the crest of the Duke of Norfolk. A medallion in another announces the name of the railway company.

The 40 arches of Sheffield's Wicker Arches, one of the city's most magnificent feats of Victorian civil engineering, were completed in 1848 as part of a viaduct to carry the rolling stock of the Manchester, Sheffield and Lincolnshire Railway high above the River Don. Their chief engineer, Sheffield-born William Fowler, went on to become the chief designer of the Forth Bridge. The stone, locally sourced, was quarried from Wharncliffe Crags.

This bridge, its blocks of shaped stone all pocked and pitted, has seen some punishment in its time. In 2007, during the second great Sheffield flood, water rose to a height of several feet at its base. One man died nearby trying to get out of his car. In June 1940, a bomb struck during the Sheffield blitz. Stand beneath the arch and peer up. What a botched job was made of the repair! To the right of the arches, on higher ground, the Victoria Hotel reminds us that there was once a well-used station here where you caught the train to Manchester. In 1963, at the station buffet, the poet Philip Larkin once ate a pie that he described as awful in a poem called 'Dockery and Son'. Behind locked gates just to the side of the arches, you can still see the flight of stone steps up to the platform.

Address The Wicker, S3 | **Getting there** Bus 52 or 52a (direction Woodhouse) from Arundel Gate to near Wicker Arches; tram to Ponds Forge / Fitzalan Square, then walk down Haymarket and Waingate, and cross Lady's Bridge onto Wicker | **Hours** Unrestricted | **Tip** Walking towards the arches from the town centre on the right-hand side of the road, you will spot a small turn to your right just before the stone steps. That little alley will lead you to a lovely suspended bridge on the Five Weirs Walk fondly known locally as the Spider Bridge.

106 __ Wincobank Hill
The cleansing of ancient ground

'All changed, changed utterly: A terrible beauty is born.' When the Irish poet W. B. Yeats wrote those words, he was referring to the heroes of the Easter Rising in Dublin, which took place in the summer of 1916. The selfsame words could equally well describe the transformation of a place in north-east Sheffield called Wincobank Hill. Sixty years ago that hill, which overlooks the Don Valley, where much of Sheffield's steel production was once located, was a miserable stretch of tawny rising ground – its colour was that of a dusty lion's pelt. Though a natural feature, it looked more like a slag heap than a hill. Almost bereft of vegetation, with the exception of a few plucky dwarf oaks clinging on for dear life, its western slope was part-covered by a random patchwork of poor-quality, post-war, prefabricated housing.

What had caused this to happen? Pollution. Almost nothing would grow in such conditions. When black soot flecks fell from the air onto crisply laundered sheets hanging out on washing lines in Sheffield's backyards, womenfolk would run out in near panic to pluck them in. Who wants to launder a sheet twice over?

Now, as you ride on the top deck of the bus down towards Fir Vale bottom, your eye, rising up beyond, catches a glimpse of Wincobank Hill today, and all is indeed changed utterly. Now that hillside is as covered with trees as any mountain in the Catskills. It is a nature reserve these days, and at its summit there are other surprises too. There is the site of an Iron Age hill fort, the line of the Roman Ridge. And then there is the view beyond, down into the Don Valley itself. Where black smoke once belched into a pitilessly polluted sky, there is now an unimpeded view of fresh awakenings: the English Institute of Sport, the Mercedes Benz factory, new housing. A blighted, soot-blackened face has been well and truly scrubbed clean.

Address 431 Jenkin Road, S5 6AQ, www.wincobankhill.btck.co.uk | Getting there Bus 3 from Arundel Gate or Meadowhall to the top of Newman Road, then a 5-minute walk uphill to the main entrance and the footpath | Hours Unrestricted | Tip Just over the crest of Jenkin Road, directly after the plaque announcing Wincobank Hill, you will spot 'Air Raid Night', a remarkable poem by a schoolgirl called Bryn Wainright on a stone column.

107 The Winter Garden

Tropical vegetation in the inner city

Is it possible for a child to swoon with contentment over a giant, heated indoor garden? Leaning back from her mother's chair, the little girl is looking upside-down at the blue sky above her head through a great sweep of curving glass as her parent sips at a coffee. The sight is indeed an extraordinary one: this great, glass-roofed oasis of calm and gentle recreation at the city's heart, populated with islands of tropical trees, shrubs, flowers, ribbed with great wooden spars that sweep up from floor to ceiling and then down again, resembles a soaring, upturned boat. Around one side of its perimeter there are various shops and cafes, encouraging you to sit and linger at one of the tables beside the huge windows which overlook Tudor Square, where you can stare at a silver birch stirring in the wind. (The Lyceum and the Crucible, Sheffield's main city-centre theatres, beckon you from the square's bottom corner.) Inside, there's Zooby's Sandwich Deli to be sampled, where you warm your hands around a nourishing cup of squash and sweet potato soup, or, for impulsive shoppers with unpredictable tastes, Sheffield Makers, a shop with a bewilderingly diverse range of local products, from line prints to lamp shades, from cocoa to playing cards. Some of the city centre's best museums are just the push of a door away: the Millennium Gallery, the Ruskin Collection.

Having finished the soup, wander past the Winter Garden's range of exotic vegetation, chosen from some of the world's most far-flung regions, which often rises high enough to challenge the slow-turning ceiling fans. Here it is all about looking – and learning too. Each island takes you to a slightly different location. You move from the Norfolk Island Pine and New Zealand flax to samples of bamboo, with a plaque singing its praises for a thousand and one uses, which range from foodstuff to scaffolding.

Address 90 Surrey Street, S1 2LH | Getting there 10-minute walk from Sheffield Interchange; tram to Castle Square and then 5-minute walk; or car: Q Park Charles Street car park | Hours Mon–Sat 8am–6pm, Sun 10am–5pm | Tip Coles Corner, a favourite meeting place for lovers, celebrated in song by Sheffield's Richard Hawley, is five minutes' walk from here, at the bottom of Fargate.

108_ Wisewood Cemetery
The death of a Leppard

Should we really expect a young rock idol to rest in peace? Jim Morrison's grave at Père Lachaise Cemetery in northern Paris seems far from at peace. Bedaubed with paint, it looks as unruly, energy-charged and visually noisy as any cherished memories of his live performances. Jim went out with a blaze. He blazes on even in death.

But Wisewood Cemetery, in the rural set-apartness of the Loxley Valley, the resting place of Def Leppard guitarist Steve Clark, is not Père Lachaise, in look or atmosphere. Unlike even Sheffield's General Cemetery, it is not a place given over to eye-catching civic pomp at all. There are no grand monuments here, nothing attention-grabbing. This place is very calm, low-lying and modestly understated. As you enter its grounds and look around, you could easily mistake it for the wide sweep of an untroubled field or a mown lawn as it declines gently down-valley towards the River Loxley itself. That river, so relatively small and unthreatening now, once came surging down through a narrow gorge into Malin Bridge and beyond, causing death on a terrible scale.

The headstones, all relatively small in size and low-lying, are organised in semicircular sweeps, with avenues between to enable you to find your way. No one has been singled out for vainglorious attention. The memories are in the freshness of flowers and the whispered messages from the living.

And that is exactly what has happened here, at the black marble headstone where we remember Steve, that fiery young guitar thrasher, who died at the age of 30 on 8 January, 1991. There are lilies, buckets of geraniums, commemorative plectrums from the band, and a hand-written letter, protected by polythene against too easy shredding by rain, which reads: 'Our beloved Steve, You'll always live in our hearts, you God of Rock.' Five Hungarian Girls have signed it.

A SWAN SONG

In Memory of

STEVE M. CLARK

A DEARLY LOVED SON AND BROTHER
WHO DIED 8TH JAN. 1991,
AGED 30 YEARS.
MEMORIES ARE TREASURES,
FRAGRANT AND SWEET,
TO CHERISH, TO HOLD,
FOREVER TO KEEP.

Address Loxley Road, S6 4TD | Getting there Bus 31 or 31a from Angel Street to Rodney Hill or Loxley Road; or car: take A61 (Barnsley), then B6077 (Loxley Road), parking inside cemetery | Hours Mon–Sat 8am–6pm, Sun 10am–5pm | Tip The Supper Spot in nearby Malin Bridge sells uncompromising Pukka-Pies.

109 Wortley Hall

Welcome to the workers' stately home

The stately home on the fringe of Sheffield called Wortley Hall looks every inch a rich man's property: the spread of its lawns; its beautifully manicured topiary; the finely stuccoed ceilings of its handsomely proportioned rooms. Beyond the woods you can hear the gentle pock-pock of a late-morning pigeon shoot.

And yet it is not. Originally a 16th-century manor house, it later became the family seat of the Earls of Wharncliffe. Occupied by the army during World War II, the house fell into disrepair. The earl, with some reluctance, offered a tenancy to local trade unionists as a place for education and recreation. Volunteers worked tirelessly to refurbish it. One of the consequences of the change of ownership that happened in 1951 is that it is likely to be the only house-cum-hotel of this kind which has copies of the *Morning Star,* a newspaper founded by the Communist Party of Great Britain in 1930, on the side tables beneath a chandelier in the principal corridor. A mahogany dresser opposite displays combative trade union leaflets: *It's GMB What's Won It!* and *Dole Not Coal* DVDs are available from reception at £5 each.

Entire wings are named after radicals of the Left. In the Robert Owen Wing an image of Karl Marx is captioned in Cyrillic. On the ground floor, the Sylvia Pankhurst Library is in regular use for trade union conferences and meetings. The library contains important texts of the Left: *Civil War in Russia; Industrial Democracy.* The walls are full of paintings, photographs, posters of the struggle to build a fairer world, including a mass meeting in Trafalgar Square, with blue, red and white pennants flying.

Each of the principal rooms is endowed by a different trade union. The Lounge, for example, was the gift, made in February 1954, of the Amalgamated Engineering Union. A plaque summarises its message: …labour the creator of wealth is entitled to all that it creates.

Address Wortley, S35 7DB, +44 (0)114 288 2100, www.wortleyhall.org.uk, info@wortleyhall.org.uk | Getting there Bus 29 (infrequent) from Sheffield Interchange to Wortley Arms, Wortley, then cross road and walk down driveway; train to Silkstone Common; or car: take A 61 from city centre, A 616 and A 629, then follow signs for Wortley Hall, on-site parking | Hours Mon – Sat 7am – 9pm | Tip Wortley Top Forge, a fine example of a 17th-century forge and ironworks with a marvellous collection of old tools and machines, is five minutes' drive from here.

110 Wyming Brook

Sheffield's miniature Alpine interlude

Greater Sheffield is a place of topographical drama: sudden vistas open out across steep-sided valleys; narrow seams of ancient woodland appear beside a road; there are more trees within its sprawling boundaries than in any other city in Europe – you will find Europe's second-longest avenue of lime trees in Sheffield, for example. Here, at Wyming Brook, a sudden turn-off from a reservoir bordered by beeches and conifers takes you to a light-dappled track wide enough to be an ancient road. There are enough strewings of pine nuts underfoot to keep any crossbill – yes, you can spot that rarity here from time to time – happy. Then, spotting a sign, you veer left off that track through a gap in an old wall, and you are quickly into a very different landscape altogether. As you begin the climb, a heath-spotted orchid shows itself at the border of a scrap of meadow. There are other natural delights too: wood sorrel, starry moss and, eventually, bushes with wild raspberries for the picking – if you are lucky enough to be here in early summer.

Then the exhilarating part begins: a climb that winds and rises precipitously, up and up, and during which you are often in dramatic sight of the thunderous downward gush of Wyming Brook itself, which seems, such is its force, to be sculpting the very rocks it flows between. The going is hard, twisty and often difficult, obliging you to take steep upward steps from one outcrop of millstone grit to another, but my god, this is nothing less than a miraculous snatch of pure Alpine scenery transported to the north of England. When you reach the top, you are bordering heathland abutting moorland, with its luxurious ferns. The walking is easier now, the views down the valley towards the stumpy brown tower blocks of the suburb of Stannington magnificent – but tread warily. Don't get caught out by a slippery tree root across the track.

Address Off Redmires Road, Peak District National Park, S10 4QX, www.wildsheffield.com/reserves/wyming-brook | Getting there No direct link on public transport: bus 51 from High Street to Lodge Moor terminus, then approximately 1-mile walk along Redmires Road; or car: take A 57 (Glossop) from city centre to Crosspool, turn left onto Sandygate Road and continue along Redmires Road, Wyming Brook car park | Hours Unrestricted | Tip Fox Hagg, a tiny nature reserve on a hillside, is just a mile from here. Take your binoculars with you for a possible sighting of a wood warbler, a crossbill or a dipper.

111_ The Zion Graveyard

Mary Anne Rawson's Resting Place

Just over the brow of Wincobank Hill (107), there was once a great house called Wincobank Hall. This had been the home of Mary Anne Rawson (1801–1887), the great campaigner against slavery in the colonies and her sister Anne Read. As a young woman in the 1820s, Rawson canvassed house-to-house, distributing tracts and pamphlets and raising money. Even in the immediate aftermath of her death in 1882, Rawson's name was already being forgotten. Her funeral report recorded these rather melancholy words: 'better known in previous times'.

Yes, it was not until as recently as 2017, almost one hundred and fifty years later, that her grave was discovered in the family vault within a tiny, overgrown, triangular graveyard once attached to a dissenting chapel in Attercliffe, hemmed in by parked cars, an auto electric shop (previously the Zion Sabbath School), and a massage parlour or two.

The Zion Graveyard is a sequestered place, freshly rescued from oblivion by local heritage enthusiasts, where nature, ever rampant, has had its way for decades. The painfully narrow entrance to the graveyard itself is to be found at the point where Zion Lane meets Lawrence Street. To find the great slab of inscribed stone that marks Rawson's family vault, you need to pick your way, very carefully and on very uneven ground, past dead nettles, mug wort, rosebay willow herb, white bryony and the fiercely tenacious bindweed, to name just a few. Someone murmurs to a passing child, 'Never climb an elder tree such as this one because its limbs are far too brittle.' And, as you go past the tottering tombstones and the rusted, collapsing ironwork – you'll see that much of the ivy has been stripped away, leaving ghostly white lines to mark its former presence. You pay your respects to the Victorian residents underground: the copper plate printer, the boot maker, the manager of the local steelworks.

Address Zion Lane, Sheffield, S9 3WD, +44 (0)7980 143776, www.ziongraveyard.chessck.com, ziongraveyard@gmail.com | Getting there Bus 52/52a from Arundel Gate; tram to Attercliffe from Sheffield or Meadowhall | Hours 2–4pm second Sunday of the month or by appointment | Tip From Zion Graveyard, walk through nearby Attercliffe Cemetery to join Five Weirs round walk and take in the River Don and the Tinsley Canal.

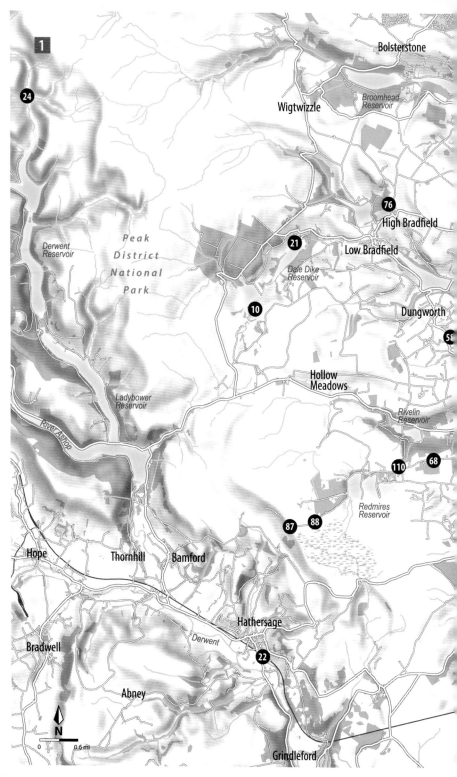

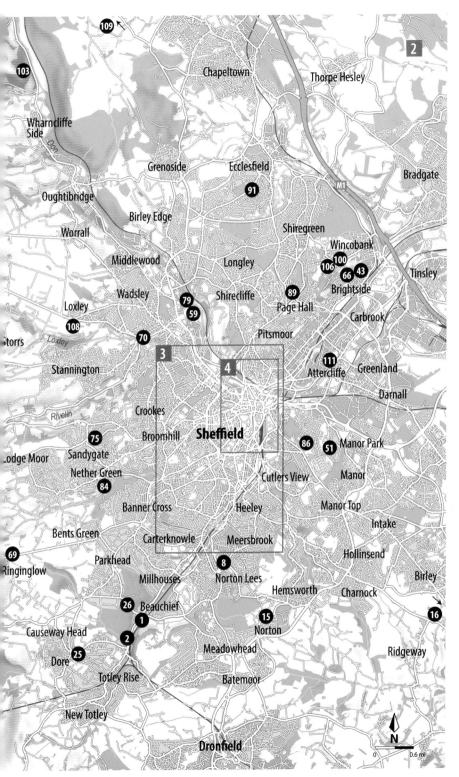

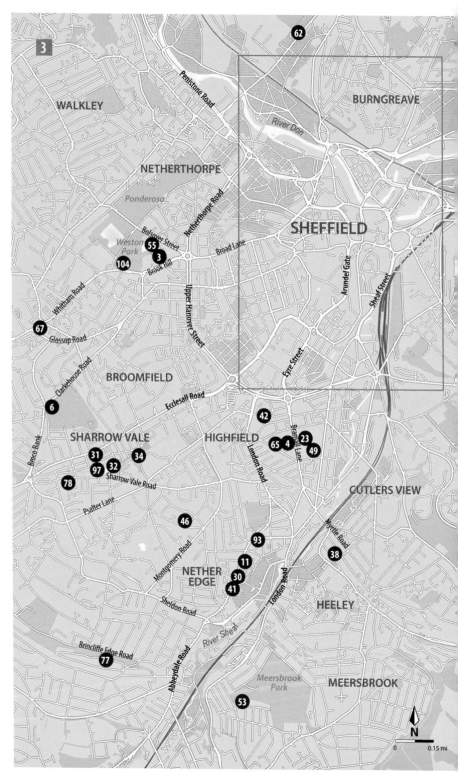

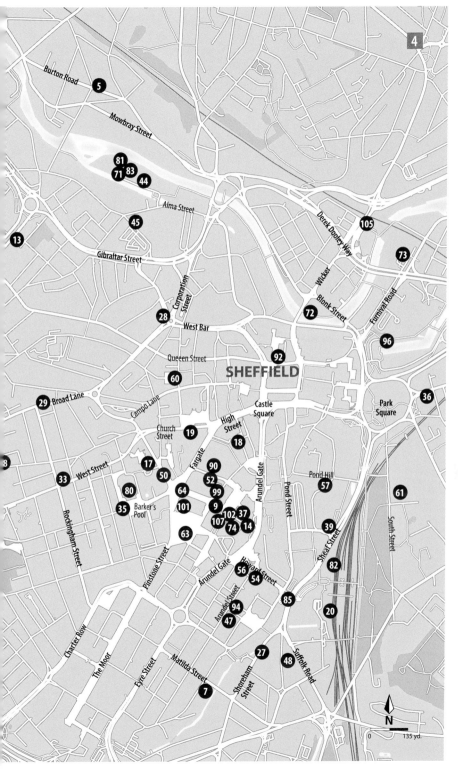

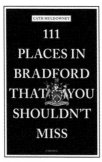

Cath Muldowney
**111 Places in Bradford
That You Shouldn't Miss**
ISBN 978-3-7408-1427-4

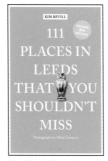

Kim Revill, Alesh Compton
**111 Places in Leeds
That You Shouldn't Miss**
ISBN 978-3-7408-2059-6

Julian Treuherz,
Peter de Figueiredo
**111 Places in Manchester
That You Shouldn't Miss**
ISBN 978-3-7408-2246-0

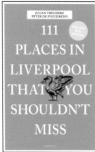

Julian Treuherz,
Peter de Figueiredo
**111 Places in Liverpool
That You Shouldn't Miss**
ISBN 978-3-7408-1607-0

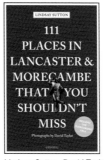

Lindsay Sutton, David Taylor
**111 Places in Lancaster
and Morecambe That
You Shouldn't Miss**
ISBN 978-3-7408-1996-5

David Taylor
**111 Places in Newcastle
That You Shouldn't Miss**
ISBN 978-3-7408-1043-6

Ed Glinert, David Taylor
**111 Places in Yorkshire
That You Shouldn't Miss**
ISBN 978-3-7408-1167-9

Katherine Bebo, Oliver Smith
**111 Places in Poole
That You Shouldn't Miss**
ISBN 978-3-7408-0598-2

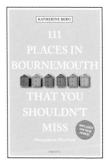

Katherine Bebo, Oliver Smith
**111 Places in Bournemouth
That You Shouldn't Miss**
ISBN 978-3-7408- 1166-2

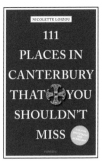

Nicolette Loizou
**111 Places in Canterbury
That You Shouldn't Miss**
ISBN 978-3-7408-0899-0

Philip R. Stone
**111 Dark Places in England
That You Shouldn't Miss**
ISBN 978-3-7408-0900-3

John Sykes, Birgit Weber
**111 Places in London
That You Shouldn't Miss**
ISBN 978-3-7408-2379-5

Ed Glinert, Marc Zakian
**111 Places in London's
East End That You
Shouldn't Miss**
ISBN 978-3-7408-0752-8

Solange Berchemin,
Martin Dunford, Karin Tearle
**111 Places in Greenwich
That You Shouldn't Miss**
ISBN 978-3-7408-1107-5

Nicola Perry, Daniel Reiter
**33 Walks in London
That You Shouldn't Miss**
ISBN 978-3-7408-1955-2

Kirstin von Glasow
**111 Gardens in London
That You Shouldn't Miss**
ISBN 978-3-7408-0143-4

Laura Richards, Jamie Newson
**111 London Pubs and Bars
That You Shouldn't Miss**
ISBN 978-3-7408-0893-8

Emma Rose Barber,
Benedict Flett
**111 Churches in London
That You Shouldn't Miss**
ISBN 978-3-7408-0901-0

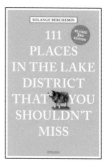

Solange Berchemin
**111 Places in the Lake District
That You Shouldn't Miss**
ISBN 978-3-7408-1861-6

Rob Ganley, Ian Williams
**111 Places in Coventry
That You Shouldn't Miss**
ISBN 978-3-7408-1044-3

Martin Booth, Barbara Evripidou
**111 Places in Bristol
That You Shouldn't Miss**
ISBN 978-3-7408-2001-5

Alexandra Loske
**111 Places in Brighton and
Lewes That You Shouldn't Miss**
ISBN 978-3-7408-1727-5

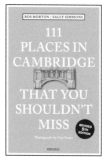

Rosalind Horton,
Sally Simmons, Guy Snape
**111 Places in Cambridge
That You Shouldn't Miss**
ISBN 978-3-7408-1285-0

Justin Postlethwaite
**111 Places in Bath
That You Shouldn't Miss**
ISBN 978-3-7408-0146-5

Gillian Tait
**111 Places in Edinburgh
That You Shouldn't Miss**
ISBN 978-3-7408-1476-2

Tom Shields, Gillian Tait
**111 Places in Glasgow
That You Shouldn't Miss**
ISBN 978-3-7408-2237-8

Gillian Tait
**111 Places in Fife
That You Shouldn't Miss**
ISBN 978-3-7408-1740-4

Acknowledgements

I wish to thank many other Sheffielders (some of them honorary) too, without whose help this book would not have been possible. I shall list them in alphabetical order: Haydn Anderson, Neil Anderson, Eddie Andrew, Dave Aspinall, Cheryl Bailey, Janet and Philip Barnes, Howard Bayley, Ann Beedham, Anthony Bennett, Tim Birkhead, Leo Birtwhistle, Jon Bradley, Trevor Brathwait, Joyce Bullivant, Alan Cordwell, Sally Clark, David Clarke, Laura Claveria, Ron Clayton, Berlie Doherty, Dan Cook, Alan Cordwell, Julie and Becky English, Catherine Flannery, Bob Franklin, John Garrett, Sally Goldsmith, Anne Goodchild, Stuart Green, John Hamshere, Paul Harbord, Ian Hargreaves, Mick and Kay Hawker, Chris Hobbs, Brian Holmshaw, James Hope-Gill, Toby Hyam, Claire Jarvis, Gina Kalsi, Steven Kay, Peter Law, James Lock, Malcolm Nunn, Ruth Nutter, Tim Nye, Calvin Payne, Dave Perry, Penny Rea, Ronay Robinson, Sally Rodgers, Nick Roscoe, Emma Paragreen, Glen Ruddiforth, Barry Short, Nigel Slack, Trevor Stacey, Kim Streets, Claire Thornley, Professor Vanessa Toulmin, Ian Turner, Alison Twells, Helen Ullathorne, Wendy Ulyett, Clive Wilmer, Linda West, Marie-Joelle West and David Westaway, Mitchell Wilson and Kane Yeardley. – *Michael Glover*

I wish to thank Stella Hunt and Mount St. Mary's College for their help and support. – *Richard Anderson*

All transport information is accurate at time of going to press. For the most up-to-date information on public transport in Sheffield and South Yorkshire, please visit www.travelsouthyorkshire.com or call South Yorkshire Traveline on +44 (0)1709 515151.

Michael Glover is a Sheffield-born, London-based poet, art critic, editor and publisher who has contributed regularly to *The Times*, the *Financial Times*, the *New Statesman* and *The Economist*. He was born in Fir Vale, Sheffield, was educated at Firth Park Grammar School, and read English at Queens' College, Cambridge. He has been a London correspondent for *ARTnews*, New York. His on-line, international poetry journal, *The Bow-Wow Shop* (www.bowwowshop.org.uk) first went online in 2009. His most recent books are: *Great Works: Encounters with Art* (Prestel), *Only So Much* (his seventh collection of poetry) and *Headlong into Pennilessness*, a memoir of growing up in Sheffield. Two collections of poetry are coming soon: *Hypothetical May Morning* and *The Book of Extremities*.

Richard Anderson is a director, writer, producer, musician and photographer, who's contributed to various media including, News International, BBC, and *Loaded Magazine*. In a previous life Richard worked for one of the world's leading PR firms, Weber Shandwick, prior to setting up his own consultancy working primarily with central Government. Sheffield-born Richard read Ancient History at London and Reading University before working across the globe. Currently he tries to focus time between his creative work, not least with sw4film.com, and work as a business mentor for the Prince's Trust.